THE

ISRAEL

DECREE

AMIR TSARFATI

HARVEST PROPHECY
AN IMPRINT OF HARVEST HOUSE PUBLISHERS

Unless otherwise indicated, all Scripture verses are taken from the New King James Version®. Copyright © 1982 by Thomas Nelson. Used by permission. All rights reserved.

Verses marked esv are taken from the ESV® Bible (The Holy Bible, English Standard Version®), copyright © 2001 by Crossway, a publishing ministry of Good News Publishers. Used with permission. All rights reserved. The ESV text may not be quoted in any publication made available to the public by a Creative Commons license. The ESV may not be translated in whole or in part into any other language.

Cover design by Bryce Williamson

Cover images © FrankRamspott / Getty Images; railway fx, DanaNguyen / Shutterstock

Interior design by KUHN Design Group

For bulk, special sales, or ministry purchases, please call 1-800-547-8979.
Email: CustomerService@hhpbooks.com

The Israel Decree
Copyright © 2025 by Amir Tsarfati
Published by Harvest House Publishers
Eugene, Oregon 97408
www.harvesthousepublishers.com

ISBN 978-0-7369-9158-2 (pbk)
ISBN 978-0-7369-9159-9 (eBook)

Library of Congress Control Number: 2024946101

Printed in the United States of America

25 26 27 28 29 30 31 32 33 / BP / 10 9 8 7 6 5 4 3 2 1

I dedicate this book to the all-powerful God who has laid out a path for me, then given me the faith to walk it. To You alone goes all the glory.

I also dedicate this book to my people and to our land. God made a promise to us thousands of years ago, and He is still holding to that promise today. You and I are the evidence of that truth. My prayer is that you will not only recognize Him for the mighty God that He is, but that you will recognize that He wants a close relationship with you, a relationship that can be found in Yeshua the Messiah.

Finally, I dedicate this book to the brave advocates who stand up for Israel day and night, and who don't let deception and confusion weaken their resolve. May they all experience a personal encounter with the Messiah of Israel and believe in Him as their Lord and Savior.

ACKNOWLEDGMENTS

First and foremost, I want to thank the Lord for His faithfulness through this last year and a half. You protected my family, and You protected me as my nation was at war. What a blessing it is to recognize that You are the One who fights our battles.

I want to thank Steve Yohn for his assistance in writing this book. I am so grateful for his ability to take my thoughts and put them down on paper.

I want to thank my wife, Miriam, my four children, and my daughter-in-law. Even through the hard times, we have remained strong as a family. I am so blessed to have you.

I want to thank my team at Behold Israel for their love, support, and dedication—Mike, H.T. and Tara, Gale and Florene, Donalee, Joanne, Nick and Tina, Jason, Abigail, Kayo, Rebecca, and Steve. You are the backbone of this ministry, and your commitment to follow God's will is what keeps us on the right track.

Special thanks to the many translators who have made my YouTube messages available in 20 different languages. Also, I offer great thanks to the many ministry coordinators around the globe who ensure everything runs smoothly at our conferences.

Thank you to Bob Hawkins Jr., Steve Miller, Kim Moore, and the wonderful team at Harvest House for all your hard work in making this book happen.

Finally, thank you so much to the hundreds of thousands of followers, prayer partners, and ministry supporters of Behold Israel. This ministry would not exist without you.

CONTENTS

THE DILEMMA WE FACE

I t's a beautiful spring morning. You're the first one up in the house and you pad into the kitchen in your slippers. After a quick grind of your coffee, you tamp rich, brown powder into your espresso machine. As you wait for the dark brown liquid to trickle into the waiting cup, you think about your day. It's going to be a good one. Plenty to do at the office, and all of it is good. The anticipation is building for your first sip of the day as you froth a little milk and pour it over your espresso. The aroma hits you as you lift the cup toward your lips, but before you get that first sip, the sirens go off.

Rockets! Inbound!

The diminutive mug is firmly planted back onto the counter as you begin to call out to your family. "Everybody up! We've got to get to the bomb shelter! Hurry, there's not much time!"

Quickly, you see doors open, and you count the family members who are rushing out. Once everyone is accounted for, you follow behind, making sure that no pets have been forgotten in the hustle. The shelter is cold and hard, but it is safe. As you sit there, you nervously joke with your family, all the while praying that the next blast of sound you hear will be the all-clear and not an explosion. Meanwhile, your cup of espresso cools on the kitchen counter, forgotten.

WHOSE LAND IS IT?

Welcome to my life and that of a great majority of Israelis. Whether or not we will still be in a state of war when you read this, I don't know. But we are certainly in one now. As wars go, this is one of the more controversial ones. There are those who say we have no right to be fighting as we are. In fact, we don't even deserve to be living where we're living. "Jews, under the auspices of Zionism, came in and stole the land from the hapless Palestinians, then tossed those rightful owners out so they became international refugees."

In contrast, many amongst the globe's population believe we are justified in carrying out this war. Yet even within this camp there are splits. Some believe that we need to go all out and finish the job, no matter what it takes. Others feel that our responses in Gaza and Lebanon are overkill. We need less bombs and more humanitarian aid. And, while you're at it, would you mind firing around the human shields so that you're hitting only the bad guys?

Another question divides the pro-war and even some of the anti-war groups. If Israel truly does belong in the land, then why? Is it due to right of conquest? Did the people buy it up legally? Did the United Nations mandate that affirmed their ownership make it theirs? Or is it something deeper, something biblical, something divine? This divide extends even into the church. Some point to the Abrahamic covenant, saying, "See, God gave this land to Abraham's descendants—the Jews, also known as Israel." Others counter, saying, "Sure, He did at one time, but the people of Israel, through their idolatry and unbelief, nullified that covenant." Or even, "You're right, the land was forever given to 'Abraham's descendants.' But those two words may not mean what you think they mean."

Here is where we find the crux of this book. When we look at Scripture, there is one reason why the Jews are in Israel: God has given that land to them. In fact, He even gave the descendants of Abraham that very name. When Jacob was about to meet his older, estranged brother, Esau, after years earlier cheating him out of his birthright and blessing, God took the opportunity to first prepare the younger sibling. The night before the potential conflict, the Lord came in a theophany, or a human manifestation, and held a wrestling match with the patriarch. After God had bested Jacob by putting his hip out of socket, we read of Him giving His opponent a new name:

> [God] said, "Let Me go, for the day breaks." But [Jacob] said, "I will not let You go unless You bless me!" So He said to him, "What is your name?" He said, "Jacob." And He said, "Your name shall no longer be called Jacob, but Israel; for you have struggled with God and with men, and have prevailed" (Genesis 32:26-28).

Israel is the Jews and the Jews are Israel. There is no difference. And those Jewish people are of the same heritage and ethnicity as the ones in the times of the patriarchs, of the wilderness wanderings, of the united kingdom, of the divided kingdom, of the exile, of the post-exile, of the time of Jesus, of the early church, of the Middle Ages, of the Ottoman Empire and the British Mandate, and now into the reconstituted State of Israel. There is no break of ownership. There is no shifting of people groups. The people of the promise that was given to Abraham are the same people who are populating Israel today.

Is modern Israel fulfilling the hope found in the Israel Decree given to the great patriarch in Genesis 12:1-3? Yes and no. But we'll get to that later in the book. Undoubtedly, however, if Abraham were to walk through the streets of today's Tel Aviv, it is very likely that he would slap his forehead and say, "*Oy vavoy!* What have I begat?" But neither the sins of today nor the sins of the past are enough to negate a promise of God. As Paul wrote to the Romans, "For what if some did not believe? Will their unbelief make the faithfulness of God without effect? Certainly not! Indeed, let God be true but every man a liar" (Romans 3:3-4).

But there are many in the church who do not believe this. They either say that God's promise to Abraham was conditional or that it was only spiritual or that it was all part of a grand scheme to do a "God's chosen" quick swap with the advent of the church age. This doctrine continues to spread rapidly through the body of Christ, and it is not new. There have been many in the history of the church who have been doing all they can to erase the ongoing importance of Israel.

QUESTIONABLE BEGINNINGS

From the beginning of the church, antisemitic Gentiles have been seeking to remove Israel from God's ongoing plans. Maybe it was because of history or jealousy, or simply because some of the Jews in the church—especially those kosher-eating, feast-keeping, circumcision-bragging, legalistic Judaizers—could be so condescending and holier-than-thou. Whatever the cause, we know this view arose early on, because we find Paul addressing it, once again, to the Romans, writing, "I say then, have they stumbled that they should fall? Certainly not! But through their fall, to provoke them to jealousy, salvation has come to the Gentiles. Now if their fall is riches for the world, and their failure riches for the Gentiles, how much more their fullness!" (11:11-12).

Have the Jews stumbled? Undoubtedly, and they're still stumbling like a drunk man trying to make his way across a rocky stream bed. But they've not fallen completely out of God's favor, which is why it will be that much more spectacular when, through faith in Yeshua, they regain their feet and finally become the witness to the world that they were originally created to be!

As much as Paul tried to tamp down the growing doctrine that claimed that Israel was replaced by the church in God's plan, it continued to spread, at times evolving into outright antisemitism. We can see the evolution within the early church fathers.

In the early second century, Justin Martyr asserted the replacement of Israel, saying, "For the true spiritual Israel [a term never found in the Bible] and descendants of Judah, Jacob, Isaac, and Abraham…are we who have been led to God through this crucified Christ…"[1] "Christ is the Israel and the Jacob, even so, we… are the true Israelitic race."[2] True, that sounds a little innocent. But it laid a foundation of Jewish nullification that later church fathers ran with.

Irenaeus, later in the second century, wrote that "they who

boast themselves as being of the house of Jacob and the people of Israel, are disinherited from the grace of God."[3] Origen,
not many years later, wrote, "We say with confidence that [the
Jews] will never be restored to their former condition. For they
committed a crime of the most unhallowed kind, in conspiring
against the Savior of the human race...and [as a result] the invi-
tation to happiness offered them by God [is] to pass to others—
the Christians!"[4] In Origen's words, we see spelled out the reason
for the rejection of Israel. The people conspired against the Messiah. But did they? Sure, some of them did. But what about the
disciples, or Jesus' family, or the thousands who were healed by
His touch? Did they conspire against Him? More about this later.

Anti-Jewish sentiment steamrolled from that point onward.
At the Council of Elvira at the beginning of the fourth century, Christians were prohibited from marrying Jews or having
a meal with them. St. John Chrysostom of the late fourth century preached a series of sermons in which he declared, "The
synagogue is not only a brothel and a theater; it also is a den of
robbers and a lodging for wild beasts..."[5] "Are [the Jews] not
inveterate murderers, destroyers, men possessed by the devil?...
Why are the Jews degenerate? Because of their hateful assassina-
tion of Christ."[6] Once again, we see a "throw the baby out with
the bathwater" argument in which an entire race of people is
nullified because of the actions of their spiritual leaders. Is that
justified? I know there are many civilians today in Iran, Lebanon, and even some in Gaza who would not buy into that gen-
eralized type of thinking.

This hateful rationale carried through the history of the church
and, sadly, was reinforced during the Reformation. Martin Luther

demanded, in his aptly titled work *The Jews and their Lies*, "Set fire to their synagogues or schools and bury and cover with dirt whatever will not burn." Why? "This is to be done in honor of our Lord and of Christendom, so that God might see that we are Christians."[7] I'm guessing that little tidbit didn't follow a lengthy exegesis on Jesus' words, "But I say to you who hear: Love your enemies, do good to those who hate you, bless those who curse you, and pray for those who spitefully use you" (Luke 6:27-28).

Even John Calvin got into the act, writing, "[The Jews'] rotten and unbending stiff-neckedness deserves that they be oppressed unendingly and without measure or end and that they die in their misery without the pity of anyone."[8] Ouch! *Et tu*, John?

Sadly, this is the legacy that has led us to the replacement theologians of today. Do I think that most who hold to this doctrine are echoing Luther's words to burn synagogues and schools? Of course not. But they do have to come to terms with the origins and evolution of their beliefs.

This is the very same doctrinal thread that led a key Reformed theologian to write,

> The promises made to Abraham, including the promise of the Land, will be inherited as an everlasting gift only by true, spiritual Israel, not disobedient, unbelieving Israel...By faith in Jesus Christ, the Jewish Messiah, Gentiles become heirs of the promise of Abraham, including the promise of the Land...Therefore, the secular state of Israel today may not claim a present divine right to the Land, but they and we should seek a peaceful settlement not based on present divine rights,

> but on international principles of justice, mercy, and
> practical feasibility.[9]

Although this statement was written nearly 20 years before the start of our present war, it still informs the opinions of many in the church. This theologian is saying that as Christians watch the actions of Israel, it should be understood that they are not fighting for what has been promised to them by God, but what was graciously bequeathed them by the United Nations. And because they were born out of the international community, they should listen more to the international community. Israel is not fighting for God, and God is certainly not fighting for Israel.

STRIVING FOR 100 PERCENT

This replacement belief system is nothing new. Again, it's been around since the beginning of the church, and all that has changed is that it's experiencing a marked upswing. So why address it now?

Not long ago, I was with a good friend of mine. He is a Bible scholar and has done great things within the Christian world. Many look up to him for his wisdom and understanding of the Scriptures. And they should!

Our conversation covered numerous doctrinal issues, and eventually migrated to discussing Israel. We talked about the nation's history and the place that it was taking in the world today. Then he said, "You know, Amir, I am 98 percent sure that the Israel of today is the Israel of the Bible." I was floored! It's possible that he was trying to encourage me by giving Israel that high of a percentage. I can't know for sure, because I was so preoccupied attempting to figure out what could possibly be contained in that last 2 percent.

It was that conversation that ultimately led to me writing this book. I had thought of calling it *100%!*, but our publisher thought that might be a little too abstract. But that title is my goal. I wish this book could convince all in the church that the Israel of today is the same Israel that God promised to Abraham. It would be amazing if this book could 100 percent stamp out the horribly errant replacement theology with one fell swoop. But I know that's virtually impossible. If Paul couldn't do that with his letters, how could I possibly do it with this short book?

I want those who love Israel and support God's chosen nation to know, beyond a shadow of a doubt, that what they believe is absolutely true. And I also want them to be fully equipped so that they can explain the reasons for their beliefs to others. I pray that this work will get into the hands of those who are on the other side of this debate too. When you look at the scriptures mentioned in this book and you read them from a literal point of view, you will see that there is no reason there must be only Israel or the church as God's chosen people, but that we serve a both/and God who has a unique and special plan for both of His holy nations.

CHAPTER 1

A GIFT FROM THE WORLD TO THE WORLD

The day had finally arrived. You'd made it! You had been assigned a parking spot, a primo space near the front. No more back lot for you with its weeds and cigarette butts and janky cars. Forget all that! You'd worked hard to be noticed, and now your hard work was paying off. You ease your sedan into your spot with no problem. Plenty of space between you and the white lines in this lot. Stepping out, you take a moment to stretch, hoping that those making their way toward the building will notice you. Finally, you reach back in, take hold of the shoulder strap of your case, straighten up, and make your way toward your office. As you walk, you press the button of your fob. The resulting chirp-chirp sounds a lot like your car telling you, "Yeah, I see you. Well done, old friend."

Through the week, you bask in the glow of your new status. At a backyard barbecue on Saturday, you tell the other guys around the grill how nice it is to not have to dodge broken bottles and overgrown thistles in the common people's lot. Sunday night comes, and you find yourself picturing the "Reserved" sign that marks out your front-lot territory.

Monday morning arrives, and you bypass your left turn to the old parking area, turning right instead. As you pass the back rows, you see your space up ahead. But just before you reach it, a fancy sports car races past you and brakes hard in your spot.

Surely, this must be a mistake! No problem, though. Easily remedied. You pull up behind the car as the driver steps out. He's big, well-muscled.

You roll down your window. "Excuse me," you say with a little laugh. "I'm afraid there's been a mistake. Easy to happen. You see, that's my parking space."

The driver glares at you, then turns away.

That's okay, maybe he just misunderstood. "Sir, do you see the 'Reserved' sign in front? I'm the one it's reserved for. So if you wouldn't mind backing out…I mean, no harm, no foul, right?" Again, you follow up with a small chuckle.

The driver turns back to you and says, "No."

No? What does he mean, "No"? Doesn't he know how these things work? There are people who have reserved spots and those who don't. You're one of the ones who has earned your reserved spot. You're about to get out of the car to explain this to the big man, but then the other door opens. Looking like a fully erect bear cresting the top of a hill, the passenger unfolds himself from the opposite side of the car. He's the size of an NFL offensive lineman, and when he slams the car door, you can feel the blast radius in your floorboard. After giving you the stink eye, he walks to his friend, and they make their way toward the building. It's obvious that they're laughing, and it's just as obvious that they're laughing at you.

This is how many people in the world perceive the Israel/Palestine question. The Palestinians were in the land, thriving due to their hard work and industriousness. Just when they were finally making something of themselves, the Jews came along and began to drive them out. The interlopers built off the strong foundation of the Palestinians and were able to forge a new nation based on the sweat of their predecessors' brows. If anyone tried to stop them, be they other Arab countries, the United Nations, or the European Union, Israel had the big bully on the block, the United States, in their corner to shut down the complainers. All the US had to do was to send a carrier group to intimidate the complainers, or worse still, threaten to cut off aid to them, and that would shut them up.

On most college campuses, this is the story you will likely hear, particularly if you converse with the matted-hair masses of protesters. But is this really what happened? Was Palestine thriving before the outsiders came in? Are the outsiders really outsiders? And do they have any legal right to be in the land?

The answer to whether the land was thriving before the people of Israel began returning in the late nineteenth century is, "Definitely not." Palestine was a pit. Made up of desert, uncultivated land, and malarial swamps, the area between the eastern shoreline of the Mediterranean and the Jordan River was a long stretch of nothing that armies were forced to pass through to get from Africa to Eurasia or the other way around. In his 1867 travel memoir *The Innocents Abroad*, Mark Twain wrote, "There was hardly a tree or a shrub anywhere. Even the olive and the cactus, those fast friends of a worthless soil, had almost deserted the country…The only difference between the roads and the surrounding country, perhaps, is that there are rather more rocks in the roads than in the surrounding country."[10]

So, no, the land was not thriving before the Jews began to resettle. As for the second question—Are the outsiders really outsiders?—we'll deal with that in the ensuing chapters when we look at Israel's biblical and historical rights to the land. The question for this chapter is the third in our list: Does Israel have any legal right to be in the land? If it doesn't, then we are fighting a battle in which religious belief goes against international law. Israel may have a biblical right to be in the land, but it has no political standing. The people are simply interlopers, and it can be understood why so many without a knowledge of Scripture stand against them.

The truth, however, is that Israel has full legal standing to exist as an independent state exactly where it is currently situated. The international community bestowed upon the Jewish people the full right to plant themselves and thrive exactly where they are. Believe it or not, that even includes the United Nations!

So how did the Jews happen to reconstitute a nation in this land?

OUT WITH THE OTTOMANS, IN WITH THE BRITS

In the late nineteenth century, antisemitism began to worsen again in Europe. An anti-Jewish undercurrent has always existed there, but every now and then, the waves would build and wreak havoc. Pogroms broke out in Eastern Europe. Jews were persecuted and driven from their homes in Western Europe. In a grand example of this anti-Jewish attitude, Alfred Dreyfus, a French artillery officer who was Jewish, was set up and wrongly convicted of treason with the Germans in 1894 and given a life sentence on Devil's Island in French Guiana. It was only after he had spent five grueling years in harsh conditions that the real culprit was discovered. Dreyfus was brought back for a new trial. However, despite the real traitor having confessed after fleeing to London, Dreyfus was once again convicted. Paris blew up between the Dreyfusards and the anti-Dreyfusards, and the Supreme Court was forced to pardon him.

The lesson that Western European Jews learned from the Dreyfus affair was not that there are many good people amongst the bad, but that at any time and for any reason, the tide could suddenly turn against you and pull you under. Meanwhile, Eastern European Jews were learning the same lesson as they were beaten and battered and driven from their homes and their properties. It was into this situation that Theodor Herzl stepped.

Theodor Herzl was born into a Jewish family in Pest, across the Danube from Buda, in the Austrian Empire. As a lawyer and a journalist, Herzl covered the Dreyfus affair from its beginnings in 1894. He saw the way that Dreyfus was railroaded. He could feel the tide shifting. The time was rapidly coming when Europe would not be safe for Jews anymore. In 1897, Herzl established the First Zionist Congress in Basel, Switzerland, at which he was elected president. For the next seven years, the final ones of his short life, he committed himself to opening doors for Jews to make *aliyah* ("to emigrate") to their ancient homeland in what is now the State of Israel.

Aliyah didn't begin with Herzl. The people of Israel had been making their way back to their homeland for centuries. In fact, there has never been a time when the land of promise was "Jew-free." God always kept a remnant there, much as He did after the Babylonian exile in the sixth century BC. But in the years leading up to Zionism*, through its birth and growth, more and more people of Israel came home. It's estimated that between 20,000 and 30,000 arrived from the early 1880s to the turn of the twentieth century.[11] Many created *moshavot* ("farm villages") so they could band together under the extremely harsh conditions and against Arab opposition. Outside money, including that from Baron Edmond de Rothschild, helped these early settlements to survive. Contrary to modern stories of how the Jews swept in and stole the land, all of the acreage for the early settlements was purchased from Arab owners who were more than happy to sell their properties, which were worthless because they were arid desert or murky swampland.

The early settling of the land was done under the watchful eyes of the Ottoman Empire, which encouraged the Rothschild-backed Jews to come in so that they could fleece them with high taxes. This changed with World War I and the defeat of the Ottomans. The Turks were driven out of the Levant, leaving a leadership vacuum that Western Europe quickly stepped in to fill.

Britain mollified the Russians by secretly allowing them to take Constantinople, while also retaining control of the Dardanelles and the Gallipoli peninsula. Moscow said, "*Spasiba*," finished off their part in World War I, then went back home so they could launch

---

* *Zionism* is defined as "the national movement for the return of the Jewish people to their homeland and the resumption of Jewish sovereignty in the Land of Israel." ("Zionism: A Definition of Zionism," *Jewish Virtual Library*, https://www.jewishvirtuallibrary.org/a-definition-of-zionism.)

the world-changing Russian Revolution. That left Britain and France looking at a map of the Middle East, each wondering how they could trick the other side so that they could get the best piece.

In walked Sir Mark Sykes and François Georges-Picot. I'll let you guess who was English and who was French. After many hours of negotiations and possibly some rock-paper-scissors, they had the remaining part of the Ottoman Empire all divided up. Signed on May 9 and 16, 1916, the Sykes-Picot Agreement allowed for France to take Lebanon and up the Syrian coast of the Mediterranean. Britain would claim Mesopotamia and oversee what is now Iraq. As for a few remaining portions of Iraq and much of Syria, Transjordan, and Palestine, local Arab chiefs would be allowed to rule.[12] Of course, their leadership would happen under French and British supervision, because how can you really trust a government without a European to oversee it? But I digress.

All was well. The Arabs were mad at the Arabs. The Arabs were mad at the Jews. The Jews were mad at the Arabs. And the fine people of Western Europe watched it all from their nice new hotels and resorts along the Mediterranean. The only problem that remained was that, like a trickling leak that eventually swamps the garden, the people of Israel kept flowing into the land west of the Jordan. But when they came, it was with Rothschild money. So the Arabs happily continued to sell their properties, and Israel's settlements multiplied across the land.

AN INTERNATIONAL THUMBS-UP

It was into this political setting that Lord Alfred James Balfour, while serving as Britain's foreign secretary, wrote a declaration to

Lord Walter Rothschild, a noted Zionist and supporter of Jews who made aliyah. In the letter, Balfour made known the pro-Israel viewpoint that many in Britain's government held. Balfour wrote on November 2, 1917,

> His Majesty's Government view with favour the establishment in Palestine of a national home for the Jewish people, and will use their best endeavours to facilitate the achievement of this object, it being clearly understood that nothing shall be done which may prejudice the civil and religious rights of existing non-Jewish communities in Palestine, or the rights and political status enjoyed by Jews in any other country.[13]

Amazingly, in that single phrase about "religious rights," Lord Balfour summed up the heart of almost every Jew in Israel. Israeli law does not demand that Christians who move to Israel become Jewish. It does not insist that Muslims convert to Judaism. There has been enough persecution of the people of Israel around the world that we simply want a place where we can be safe from those who hate us simply because we are Jewish. And if you want to come and be a productive member of our nation, we're happy to have you, no matter what you believe.

The Balfour Declaration was very encouraging to the Jews and to the Zionist movement. Unfortunately, despite Balfour being foreign minister, it was still nothing more than a nice support letter. There were no teeth behind it; no built-in actions or next steps. It was essentially an "I wish I may, I wish I might."

Then in April 1920, representatives from the British Empire,

France, Japan, and Italy met in San Remo, Italy, with some from the United States attending as observers. Earlier, I mentioned that after the division of the post-war Ottoman Empire, Syria, much of Mesopotamia, and Jordan/Palestine were to be placed under local Arab leadership. But what would that look like, what borders would be drawn, and how would the outside powers factor into the mix? Those were the issues taken up in San Remo. Decisions were made and important agreements were signed. But in relation to the Jewish people, the key excerpt from the San Remo Resolution, ratified on April 25, 1920, reads:

> The High Contracting Parties agree to entrust, by application of the provisions of Article 22, the administration of Palestine, within such boundaries as may be determined by the Principal Allied Powers, to a Mandatory, to be selected by the said Powers. The Mandatory will be responsible for putting into effect the declaration originally made on November 8, 1917, by the British Government [the Balfour Declaration], and adopted by the other Allied Powers, in favour of the establishment in Palestine of a national home for the Jewish people, it being clearly understood that nothing shall be done which may prejudice the civil and religious rights of existing non-Jewish communities in Palestine, or the rights and political status enjoyed by Jews in any other country.[14]

In this remarkable document, the international community officially asserted its intention to allow for a Jewish national homeland in the area that was then called Palestine. Again, the goal was for Jews, Christians, and Muslims to live together in peace. The Jews were all for that. The Christians were all for that. It was and is only from large parts of the Muslim community that we hear calls of "Death to Israel," and that we read in the Hamas Covenant, "Israel will exist and will continue to exist until Islam will obliterate it, just as it obliterated others before it."[15] By the way, Hamas made its attempt to follow through with that commitment on October 7, 2023. It failed.

Many people point to the Balfour Declaration as the document that solidified Israel's future, but that foundation really emerged from San Remo. Then, the curing of that strong base took place with the Palestine Mandate, issued by the League of Nations and signed on July 24, 1922. This remarkable piece of work recognized Israel's historic, unbreakable connection with the land. It called for "the establishment of the Jewish national home" and encouraged "close settlement" for returning Jews throughout the country. All areas were open to aliyah, "including State lands and waste lands not required for public purposes."[16] If the new settlers found unclaimed land, they claimed it, then set to work bettering it. It is because of these industrious emigrees that, when I look out my back window at the Jezreel Valley, I see lush farmland instead of the malarial swamps that were originally there.

"That's fine, Amir, but that's all history. The British Mandate—gone. The League of Nations—gone. Now we're under the United Nations, and we all know the UN hates Israel." True on all points, especially the UN's seething antipathy toward my tiny country. However, in just this one small area, I'm happy to announce we even have the United Nations on our side. In the UN's original charter, which went into effect on October 24, 1945, Article 80, often referred to as the Palestine Clause, stated:

> Except as may be agreed upon in individual trusteeship agreements, made under Articles 77, 79, and 81, placing each territory under the trusteeship system, and until such agreements have been concluded, nothing in this Chapter shall be construed in or of itself to alter in any manner the rights whatsoever of any states or any peoples or the terms of existing international instruments to which Members of the United Nations may respectively be parties.[17]

Now, if you're thinking that sounds like a bunch of lawyerly gobbledygook that doesn't even mention Israel, you're exactly right. However, it was placed in the charter specifically because of the Arab objections to Israel and affirms the right of the Jews to eventually establish their own homeland. How do I know this was the intention? Because it was upheld by the International Court of Justice in 1960, 1971, and 2004. As much as the United Nations would like to take their words back, they can't. They're stuck with us because of their very own charter. I mean, that's got to hurt at least a little bit.

BIRTH OF "THE PALESTINIAN"

What about the rights of the Palestinians who were living in the land when the Jewish people started to move in and take over?

To answer that question, one must determine what exactly a Palestinian is. Prior to 1948, a Palestinian was anyone who lived in the British Mandate of Palestine, whether they were Muslim, Jew, or Christian. Not until after the State of Israel came into being was the term honed down to refer only to those Arabs in the land who chose not to become citizens of the new nation. Suddenly, out of the blue, there was a new people group.

Some of these new Palestinians stayed in Israel. Others moved to surrounding countries, such as Jordan and Syria. As soon as Israel declared its statehood and drove off the instantly invading armies, the United Nations got involved. In 1949, the United Nations Relief and Works Agency for Palestine Refugees in the Near East (UNRWA) was formed, and immediately, handouts were given to the Palestinians. Not surprisingly, as soon as the charitable support began, the Palestinian population exploded.

It takes a while for a population to double. In 2023, the world's population reached eight billion. That's twice what it was 48 years earlier in 1975. Undoubtedly, high birth rates and medical science are causing an exponential increase in the number of living people and the lengths of their lives. However, according to a 2022 statement by the chairperson of the Palestinian Central Bureau of Statistics (PCBS), "the Palestinian population at home and in the diaspora has doubled about ten times since the Nakba in 1948."[18] *Nakba* is an Arabic term that means "catastrophe" and is used of the advent of Israel's statehood and the subsequent departure of Arabs from their homes in the land.

Think about that statistic put forth by a Palestinian-sympathizing organization. According to the latest figures, worldwide, it took almost 50 years for the population to double. The Palestinians, however, have doubled their numbers ten times in 84 years. There are only two possible explanations for this near-miraculous population increase. Either the Fertile Crescent is truly the *fertile* crescent, or many Arabs from the countries surrounding Israel suddenly began identifying as Palestinian. Why would Arabs jump on the Palestine bandwagon? I mean, living as a Palestinian is not the most glamorous life. However, trying to eke out an uncertain living in many parts of Syria, Jordan, and Iraq is even less glamorous. The positive side of being Palestinian is that even if you sit around all day and do nothing, you still have UNRWA available to help make sure you have schools for your kids, food for your cupboards, and shovels for digging your terrorist tunnels.

A BOND THAT CANNOT BE BROKEN

There is a bond between the Israeli people and the land. When folks think of that connection, their minds will often go back to Abraham and Moses, King David and Jesus. But this is more than just a religious belief or a cultural history. The land belongs to Israel because the international community has said it belongs to Israel. The Jews are not invaders or interlopers. They did not drive people out, nor did they wipe off the map huge groups of innocents in genocidal attacks.

From the beginning of the first aliyah, the Jewish people began moving in with the intention of sharing the land with those already living there. But at every negotiation, with every treaty proposal, the Jews had their outstretched hands of friendship swatted away by the Arabs. This includes before and after Israel declared independence in 1948. There is nothing that Israelis want more than to be able to tear down the walls and border fences that surround their nation and live as friendly neighbors with those around them. From the beginning, though, Israel has had to constantly take a defensive posture because the surrounding countries have repeatedly stated their intention of pushing the Jews into the sea.

But that's not going to happen. First, it can't because Israel has an internationally recognized legal right to exist and dwell in the land. But more importantly, God is not going to let it happen.

CHAPTER 2

AN ETERNAL PROMISE IS MADE

Desert sand compacts under his feet. The jagged grit is in no way unpleasant, even when he feels its tiny points jab into his soles. The sensation feels familiar, comforting. He's been walking this type of ground since he was old enough to manage putting one foot in front of the other without stumbling. Stopping for a moment, he lets the cool breeze wisp through his beard and rustle his hair, bringing with it the scents of tamarisk blossoms and acacia.

It wasn't unusual for the man to find himself out walking late at night. Family struggles, rumors of raiding parties, and a general restlessness often had him leaving his tent when all others were asleep. But nothing sent him seeking solace from the moon and the stars more often than his wife's tears. On the surface, the long-married couple seemed no different than any other in their settlement. It was only at night when they retreated to their tent that the problem could be seen and heard. Or, maybe more accurately, not heard. When the flaps closed, there were only two quiet people inside. One husband, one wife. No playful giggles, no childish screams, no soft cooing. Just a man and a woman and a lot of unfulfilled dreams.

Tonight, he walked his solo sojourn into the desert, the same one he had taken so many times when he had run out of comforting words for his beloved bride. But this time was different. He recognized where he was; he just couldn't remember how he had gotten here. He couldn't even recall what might have pushed him out into the night air. There had been no rows with his brother over what to do now that their father had passed. His wife had gone to sleep early, so there had been no difficulty with her. As he thought about it, he remembered that he had been very tired that evening and had called it a night soon after the sun had set.

So, how was he now out in the desert? The wind again blew gently, bringing the familiar smells along with something new. Something aromatic, rich, lovely. With the scents, he also felt a tension building in the air, almost like a buzzing that made the hair on his arms and legs stand up. What was going on?

A brilliant light suddenly surrounded him, and a voice said, "Abram."

When a disembodied light speaks to you, there is usually only one appropriate response. Abram dropped to his knees, then stretched out prostrate. "Yes, Lord?"

When the voice spoke again, Abram could feel its resonance; he could see little bits of grit vibrating up and down at eye level. It said:

Get out of your country,
from your family
and from your father's house,
to a land that I will show you.
I will make you a great nation;
I will bless you
and make your name great;
and you shall be a blessing.
I will bless those who bless you,
and I will curse him who curses you;
and in you all the families of the earth shall
be blessed (Genesis 12:1-3).

The light then increased its intensity to the point that Abram had to squeeze his eyes tight, covering them with his hands and pushing his face into the ground. Suddenly, the brilliance disappeared. Abram took his hands away and tried to look around, but after having taken in the light's intensity, everything now was pitch black. He waited for his eyes to adjust. Even without sight, it was obvious to him that he was no longer in the desert. Instead of scrub trees and wild aromatics, he could smell years-old leather and the lingering remnants of the evening communal meal. The sounds were also different. In place of the whisper of the desert breeze, he could hear the soft snore of his sleeping wife, Sarai, on the other side of the hanging fabric divider.

Once Abram could see again, he stood from his bed, pulled on a robe, and fastened his sandals to his feet. Because it was still night, he lifted a heavy walking stick that was leaning next to the tent's exit. Pushing back the flap, he slipped out and began walking through the tent community toward the desert. The dream or vision or whatever it was had been jarring. He had a lot to process. The one thing that he was certain of was that as soon as was humanly possible, he was taking a road trip from which he would likely never return.

AN ORDINARY HERO

This, admittedly with a little dramatic flair, was the moment that the Israel Decree was first given. God looked over all the people in the world, spotted Abram, and said, "Yeah, he'll do." There was nothing special about the man. There is nothing said of his great faith in God before his calling. Joshua, when speaking to the Israelites after they had begun their conquering of the land, said, "Thus says the LORD God of Israel: 'Your fathers, including Terah, the father of Abraham and the father of Nahor, dwelt on the other side of the River in old times; and they served other gods'" (Joshua 24:2). Therefore, it's quite likely that Abram originally followed the pagan faith of his fathers. We also hear nothing about his character or his righteousness.

What is evident is that God saw in Abram a man who was ready to obey, even when the task was difficult. God told Abram to leave behind his country and his family and set out on a journey whose destination was on a need-to-know basis, and Abram didn't need to know. His response to that open-ended command tells all we need to know about his character. The first three words we read in Scripture after the Israel Decree was given are, "So Abram departed" (Genesis 12:4). Abram didn't weigh the pros and cons or seek wise counsel. He didn't pull out a map or flip a coin. As soon as was possible, he packed up the caravan and beat hoof.

This reminds me of an incident later in his life, after he had been given the new name of Abraham, an appellation we'll use for him in this book from here on in order to avoid confusion. God had finally given him the child of promise, the one from whom would come "the great nation" of the Israel Decree. But with that son, Isaac, would come one more test of Abraham's faith.

> [God] said, "Take now your son, your only son Isaac, whom you love, and go to the land of Moriah, and offer him there as a burnt offering on one of the mountains of which I shall tell you" (Genesis 22:2).

What are the next words we read after this unimaginably difficult request? "So Abraham rose early in the morning and saddled his donkey" (verse 3). Abraham completely trusted God, even when it seemed antithetical to do so. He knew that God would never go back on a promise.

> By faith Abraham, when he was tested, offered up Isaac...concluding that God was able to raise him up, even from the dead, from which he also received him in a figurative sense (Hebrews 11:17, 19).

Even if it took a resurrection miracle, God would remain true to His word. It is that same kind of faith that can get us through even the worst of times in our own lives. The Lord has shown that He will do whatever it takes, even to the extent of the crucifixion and resurrection of His own Son, to ensure that we have the opportunity to be safe with Him. What peace that should give us in our day-to-day walks!

AN EXTRAORDINARY DECREE

The Promise of the Land

Let's go back to the night of the vision. As Abraham mulled over God's words while wandering under the lights of the sky, there were a number of truths that would have stood out to him. First, only one directive was given to him, and it came in the first two words.

"Get out."

These are huge words. They're a demand for movement, like "scoot, *lech lecha*, get yourself on out of here." "Get" is a second-person singular verb, meaning the directive was given to Abraham and Abraham only. God was not saying, "Pack up the family and head off on a trip." In fact, He said the opposite. "Get out of your country, from your family and from your father's house, to a land that I will show you" (Genesis 12:1). It's great if Sarai's up for it, and your nephew, Lot, can tag along, too, if he wants. But if they say they're staying, you're still going.

Second, it was an open-ended command. As I mentioned earlier, there was no discussion of where Abraham was going to. God simply told him, "I'll let you know when you get there." The whole purpose of the command was to move Abraham from where he was to the land that God had already made the heritage of his progeny. In fact, it took only a few verses and a whole bunch of kilometers for Abraham and his gang to get down to

Shechem, which is about halfway between Jerusalem and the Jezreel Valley in modern Israel. There, God appeared to him again and said, "To your descendants I will give this land" (verse 7). What is "this land"? It is the land of Israel. Promised by God to Abraham's offspring.

This brings us to the first aspect of the Israel Decree. God has given Israel a specific piece of land.

"But, Amir, God said 'descendants.' That's an indefinite timeframe. How many generations of descendants? Maybe after all the sin and idolatry, the Lord got tired of them and took back the promise. Certainly couldn't blame Him." I would agree with most of that statement. "Descendants" can be open-ended, although it normally isn't. And, after all the sin and idolatry, I in no way could blame God for wanting to take back the heritage of the land. But He simply wouldn't do it. That's not His character. God's gift of the land to the Israelites was a permanent bequeathment.

Abraham and Lot were both materially blessed by God. The flocks and herds of each increased exponentially and the tents of their people expanded to take up more and more space. Abraham finally said to Lot, "Listen, nephew, this land isn't big enough for the two of us. We've got Canaan up here or the plains of the Jordan down below. You choose which you want." Lot looked at the rocky land above and the lush greenery below and said, "You know, I think I'll head down." I've heard it said that property values are often based on timing. Never more true than with Lot.

Abraham had done the right thing, but it still might have felt like a thumb in the eye when Lot chose the lusher area. So God came and gave Abraham a morale booster. He said:

> Lift your eyes now and look from the place where you
> are—northward, southward, eastward, and westward;
> for all the land which you see I give to you and your
> descendants forever. And I will make your descendants
> as the dust of the earth; so that if a man could number
> the dust of the earth, then your descendants also could
> be numbered. Arise, walk in the land through its length
> and its width, for I give it to you (Genesis 13:14-17).

It's that last word in the first sentence of this second install-ment of the Israel Decree that makes all the difference: "forever." It is a word of finality. There is no caveat, no asterisk. You can read this in the original language, and the meaning is still the same. You can break down the words or parse the verbs or look between the lines. There's just no way to get around "forever."

If you think about it, that word actually makes a dual prom-ise. First, it assures that the land will always belong to Israel. Sec-ond, it confirms that there will always be Jews around to live in it. "From the River to the Sea, Israel is a guarantee."

This is typically when the "what abouters" will come in and say, "Amir, what about during the exiles, when the people of Israel were either in Babylon, former Assyria, or Egypt? Weren't all the Jews driven out? And what about after the Bar Kokhba rebellion, when the Jews were expelled from the newly chris-tened Syria Palestina? If there are no Jews in Israel, then doesn't the Israel Decree fall flat?"

As I mentioned in an earlier chapter, there has always been a remnant of Jews in Israel. But ultimately, that's a nowhere argu-ment because presence doesn't prove ownership. I could refuse to leave a house I've been evicted from for not paying property taxes. Even though the house had been mine and my body was still within its walls, legally, the house would no longer belong to me.

Instead, what's most important is ownership. Let's say I bought a condominium in Haifa that I could take the family to on vacations. One day, after we leave, another family breaks in, moves in their furniture, sets out their dishes, and takes over the place. Have I lost my home just because I wasn't in it at the time? Are the other people the new owners despite me having the deed? Is possession really nine-tenths of the law?

This is where we need to take a step back to look at who really owns the land in question. In the sixth century BC the Babylonians said it was theirs. Then came the Persians to claim proprietorship. Then it was Alexander the Great and the Hellenes. After that were the Romans, then the Arabs, then the Crusaders, then the Mamluks, then the Ottomans, and then the British. All of them claimed the land belonged to them, and all of them were wrong. Bookending the list before Babylon and after the Brits was God's choice—Israel. Does that make them the true owners? Yes. Or at least yes-ish.

The owner of the land of Israel has been and always will be God. He is its Maker and He retains the rights of His creation. It doesn't matter who the current bully on the block is. It's irrelevant who has the bigger swords, faster horses, most powerful guns, or most destructive bombs. As we've already seen, God, who has full rights to the land, once said to Abraham, "All the land which you see I give to you and your descendants forever" (Genesis 13:15). Forever means forever. Any person in Israel other than a physical descendant of Abraham is just a squatter in someone else's home.

The Promise of a Nation

There is more to the Israel Decree, however, than just the land. The second promise given to Abraham is that of seed. Progeny was everything in ancient culture, and it still is in many parts of the world today. As Solomon wrote, "Like arrows in the hand of a warrior, so are the children of one's youth. Happy is the man who has his quiver full of them" (Psalm 127:4-5). Unfortunately for the great patriarch of Israel, at the time of his vision, the only things in his quiver were some wispy webs and a few dead spider husks.

Yet God made it clear to this man who was well on the downside of "prime" on life's bell curve that He would make him into "a great nation" (Genesis 12:2). It was an incredible testimony to the faith of this septuagenarian that he didn't push back on God at the end of the promise and say, "Now, about that whole 'nation' thing. You do know I'm seventy-five, right?" Remember, Abraham was no different than you or me. He was no superhero. There was no cape under his robe ready to break out and flutter in the wind. Like all of us, he had his moments of failure. Remember the two times he said his wife was his sister because he was scared? And then there was that whole Hagar incident. Oy!

What made this great patriarch stand out was his willingness to take God at His word no matter what. "I'm super old and my wife is beyond childbearing, but You say we're going to produce a great nation? Sure, why not? I'm in." So often when God challenges us or puts difficult opportunities in front of us, our first response is to question. "Can I really do it? Do I have the time? Is it within my gifting?" When God gives us opportunities and promises, He's not looking for questions. He wants to hear only one answer: "Yes."

This promise of physical descendants was important to both Abraham and God, which is why the Lord repeated it over and over. When Abraham began to doubt, God renewed the covenant:

> [God] brought [Abraham] outside and said, "Look now toward heaven, and count the stars if you are able to number them." And He said to him, "So shall your descendants be" (Genesis 15:5).

Later, when Abraham was 99 years old and still without his heir, God changed his name to emphasize the promise:

> Abram fell on his face, and God talked with him, saying: "As for Me, behold, My covenant is with you, and you shall be a father of many nations. No longer shall your name be called Abram, but your name shall be Abraham; for I have made you a father of many nations. I will make you exceedingly fruitful; and I will make nations of you, and kings shall come from you. And I will establish My covenant between Me and you and your descendants after you in their generations, for an everlasting covenant, to be God to you and your descendants after you" (17:3-7).

Finally, after the heir was miraculously born—Isaac, the son of promise—and Abraham took him to the mountain to sacrifice him according to God's command, the Angel of the Lord said:

By Myself I have sworn, says the LORD, because you have done this thing, and have not withheld your son, your only son—blessing I will bless you, and multiplying I will multiply your descendants as the stars of the heaven and as the sand which is on the seashore; and your descendants shall possess the gate of their enemies. In your seed all the nations of the earth shall be blessed, because you have obeyed My voice (22:16-18).

For Abraham, it was important to be reminded that, as the years passed, God was still on board with the plan and would bring it about in His time. For God, it was imperative that not just Abraham but everyone throughout the ensuing ages would recognize that the physical descendants of this old man were a miraculous creation brought about by His hand. Israel doesn't exist by accident or by the normal uniting of a man and woman. Israel exists because God intervened into the natural way of things and brought about the pregnancy of a woman far too old to bear children. The Jews were born through supernatural means, and they have been sustained through the millennia through supernatural means. Does this make them better than everyone else? No. But it does make them chosen, and it sets them apart as unique in God's plan.

The Promise to Be a Blessing

The third promise in the Israel Decree is that Abraham's descendants would be a blessing to the nations. In that world-changing vision, God made a declaration that would extend far beyond one man's family. He said, "I will bless you and make your name great; and you shall be a blessing. I will bless those who bless you, and I will curse him who curses you; and in you all the families of the earth shall be blessed" (Genesis 12:2-3). What an amazing promise! Notice that there is no time limitation, no geographical constraint. A blessing will come from Abraham and his posterity that will reach to all people of all time. How is that possible?

To understand the extent of the promised blessing, we need to understand the blessing itself. While there are many ways that Abraham's descendants have had a positive impact on this world, there are three primary ones worth mentioning.

BLESSING THE WORLD BY SHOWING GOD'S CHARACTER

First, the people of Abraham were set apart to be witnesses of the glory of God. Speaking to Israel, the Lord said,

> "You are My witnesses," says the LORD,
> "and My servant whom I have chosen,
>   that you may know and believe Me,
>   and understand that I am He.
> Before Me there was no God formed,
>   nor shall there be after Me.
> I, even I, am the LORD,
>   and besides Me there is no savior.
> I have declared and saved,
> I have proclaimed,
>   and there was no foreign god among you;
>   therefore you are My witnesses,"
> says the LORD, "that I am God" (Isaiah 43:10-12).

According to the plan, the descendants of Abraham were to demonstrate to the surrounding nations the power, glory, and righteousness of a holy and loving God. By looking at the character of Israel's people, the world should have gotten a glimpse of the divine. If you wanted to see God's mercy, you would only need to look at the way Abraham's descendants consistently showed mercy to the helpless and the desperate. If you wanted to see holiness, then you could simply open up the Old Testament and read about how perfectly the ancient Hebrews followed God's commands. The Lord had created Israel to be a special nation unto Himself so that the people could show His wonderful light to the world.

That was God's intention. Unfortunately, in this regard, Israel failed miserably. But more about that later.

Blessing the World by Giving the Word

Thankfully, there were two more ways that Israel could bless all people. The second gift that Abraham's progeny has given to humanity is the Word of God. It's true that the natural world gives testimony to who God is. The apostle Paul wrote that "since the creation of the world [God's] invisible attributes are clearly seen, being understood by the things that are made, even His eternal power and Godhead" (Romans 1:20). When one closely examines the intricacies of creation and the perfection of the systems in nature and within life, only a person desperate to uphold a preconceived naturalistic notion can say "randomness" and not "creator."

But general revelation was not enough for God. He wanted His creation to understand their origin, to know who He is, and, most importantly, to recognize and accept His plan for their salvation. Thus, he gathered 40 different authors from three different continents writing in three different languages over a 1,500-year time span and had them put together a book. One thing that every one of those writers had in common is that they were all Jewish. Every word in every book in both testaments came either from the pen of a descendant of Abraham or from the scribe to whom they were dictating. As the psalmist wrote:

> [God] declares His word to Jacob,
> His statutes and His judgments to Israel.
> He has not dealt thus with any nation;
> and as for His judgments, they have not known them.
> Praise the Lord! (Psalm 147:19-20).

God chose Israel to be His spokespeople. Through them, He would communicate directly to His creation. And, unlike Israel's utter failure at being God's witnesses, they knocked this one out of the park. What we now have in the Bible is the sole perfect, accurate book of divine truth. God's words put on paper.

"But, Amir, it's been two thousand years. How can we still have confidence that we can trust the Bible? Think of all the errors that have probably slipped in over that time." If you were talking about any other book, I'd be right there with you. It's impossible to copy something by hand time after time over that lengthy span and not have major discrepancies creep into the text. But this isn't any other book. This is God's Word that He chose to give to humanity.

I could go into the intricacies of the copying process. So

precise. So detailed. I could talk to you about manuscripts and archaeology and unfailing prophetic fulfillments over time and the breath-stealing statistics surrounding the never-miss nature of those unfailing prophetic fulfillments. But this is a short book, and I've written all that before.

When we talked earlier about land, we said that when you cut through all the politics and conquests and residencies, it all comes down to God. He owns the land. He gave the land. The same is true when it comes to God's Word. The overarching umbrella that covers all the other arguments about accuracy and trustworthiness is the purpose and character of God. He wanted to communicate truth to the world, so He did so. It took a millennia and a half for Him to gradually lay it all out. Many generations came and went. But eventually, the apostle John wrote the *Fin* to the Bible: "The grace of our Lord Jesus Christ be with you all. Amen" (Revelation 22:21). And it was done. Mission accomplished.

Recognizing the intricate process and understanding God's desire to be known, do you think that He would allow His one shot at communicating all necessary truth to humanity to become corrupted? Was He watching a fourth-century council sift through a pile of scrolls, saying, "Wait, don't forget about Thomas's gospel! And Tobit—you can't leave Tobit out of the Old Testament!" God undertook the greatest literary project of all time and pulled it off without a hitch. If we have any doubts, we can look back at the thousands of manuscripts from early- to middle-church years to confirm that nothing has changed. God came up with the words, He got Abraham's descendants to write them down. And the Holy Spirit has safeguarded them ever since.

Blessing the World by Producing the Savior

The final blessing to the nations in the Israel Decree is the Savior. You may not realize this after seeing the picture of the blond-haired, blue-eyed Jesus hanging in your grandmother's kitchen, but Jesus is a Jew. And what greater blessing could Abraham give to the world than to be the father of the people who would give humanity its much-needed Messiah? This is the gift above all gifts.

I love how Paul gave a quick list of all that Israel has given to humanity. He called them

> my countrymen according to the flesh, who are Israelites, to whom pertain the adoption, the glory, the covenants, the giving of the law, the service of God, and the promises; of whom are the fathers and from whom, according to the flesh, Christ came, who is over all, the eternally blessed God. Amen (Romans 9:3-5).

Notice that Paul was speaking of physical Jews, those who were his "countrymen according to the flesh." This is not the church. They aren't Gentiles made Abraham's spiritual children through a circumcision of the heart (Romans 2:25-29). As Paul said, they "are Israelites." He then walked the reader through a long list of the many benefits that Israel has given to the world. And he wrapped it up with the most important: "Christ...the eternally blessed God."

Tragically, despite the Messiah coming from Israel, most Jews don't recognize Him for who He is. As John wrote, "He came to His own, and His own did not receive Him" (John 1:11). There are those who look at John's words and take them as all-encompassing.

"Israel rejected the Messiah; therefore, God rejected Israel." But John wasn't making a blanket statement. He was generalizing. Did the majority of Jews reject the Messiah? Most definitely. But Jesus' mother didn't reject Him. Mary Magdalene and the siblings Lazarus, Martha, and Mary didn't reject Him. His disciples certainly didn't reject Him; all of them except John went to their deaths because of their commitment to Him. Even Jesus' brothers, James and Jude, finally came around to believing in Him.

But there are those who say that the sinfulness of Israel led to God breaking His covenant with the people. Their disobedience reached its pinnacle with the cries of "Crucify Him," and the Father had finally had enough. His patience came to an end, and He cut His ties with them. But thankfully, they say, the timing was perfect, because God, in His wisdom, had a brilliant plan waiting to be implemented. On the Day of Pentecost, the church was born, and God had new people to replace Israel.

Others are uncomfortable with that theory because they understand the implication of God going back on His "forever" commitments to Abraham and the people of Israel. How could we trust His forever promises of salvation and eternal life if He could pull the rug out from under the feet of the Jews? This doctrinal school of thought smooths the rough edges of Jewish rejection by saying it was God's plan all along to replace Israel with the church. Israel was established in order to lay a foundation for righteousness, sort of like holy living, but with training wheels. After the crucifixion and resurrection of Jesus, it was time to swap players. A sin-battered and bruised Israel dragged itself to the ropes and tagged in the church. Bold and energetic, this new entity leapt into the ring and accomplished what its predecessor never could.

It spread the gospel far and wide, living as a perfect(ish) reflection of Christ to the world. Great plan, Lord! We'll keep watching the world improve until the time comes for You to return and usher in the new heavens and the new earth.

Is that really what happened? Was the Israel Decree just temporary? Or did it maybe have a special, hidden meaning that could be understood with a little presupposition and some reading between the lines? Or did God's words mean exactly what they say? Does "a great nation" mean a physical "great nation"? Can we trust "forever" to mean "forever"? In the next couple chapters, it's those issues and others that will come up as we look at God's commitment to the people of Israel in the Old Testament and the New Testament.

CHAPTER 3

A SOLID FOUNDATION THAT ENDURES

The day was September 27, 2022, and I was relaxing in the hotel lobby waiting for Behold Israel's senior writer, Steve Yohn, to come down from his room. Outside, the late summer morning was already warm. We had scheduled an early breakfast so that we could beat the Fort Worth heat. In just a few days, Behold Israel would be holding an Awaiting His Return conference, and I was anticipating the time the ministry would have at one of our favorite churches.

But for now, I had other things on my mind. I had invited Steve to fly in several days early to talk about an upcoming book. This morning, we would begin our discussions, which were always both challenging and enjoyable.

When I spotted Steve exiting the elevator area, I stood to meet him. I noticed that he had a grin on his face and was shaking his head.

Reaching me, he said, "Three complete strangers on the elevator told me how sorry they are for my loss."

I gave him a curious look, and he pointed to the cap on his head, which bore a Denver Broncos logo. Then his comment made perfect sense. Just three days earlier, the Miami Dolphins had whomped the Broncos, 70 to 20, scoring the highest number of points by an NFL team since 1966.

Steve, who lives just outside of Denver, said, "It's been a brutal few days."

We went through the revolving door and headed toward the street. As we walked, I asked him what led to the Broncos' spectacular collapse.

"The best offense is a good defense," he replied. "Unfortunately, we had neither."

As I approach this next stage of the book, I can't help but think about this strategy. When you are well-defended, you are able to go after your opponent without fear of being surprised or overwhelmed. It's like establishing a strong foundation before constructing a building. Doing this works in construction. It works in sports. It also works in theology. If you have a thoroughly thought-out doctrinal position that is well supported by accurately exegeted Scripture, then you have the comfortable freedom to question the other side's positions. However, if you begin on shaky ground, lacking either scriptural support or clearly thought-out positions, then you are constantly susceptible to well-placed queries or biblical-sounding arguments.

Therefore, in these next two chapters, I intend to first present solid evidence of Israel's once-and-always place in God's plan for the world. Then second, I will look at some of the main arguments people in the replacement theology camp use to support their beliefs, explaining why they don't hold up to biblical scrutiny.

My goal is for you to walk away from this book with the assurance that Israel was God's chosen people from the moment the Israel Decree was given to Abraham, and they continue to be His chosen people as they exist in the State of Israel today. This will not change until the day when the new heavens and new earth arrive, when all distinctions are removed and everyone who belongs to God is of the same glorious heritage.

A THREE-PERSON DANCE

Why did God create the world? Because it was in His nature to do so. As a creative God, He desired an outlet to express His character. We see perfection in the systems of the world because God is a perfect God. We see beauty and symmetry and colors and variety because God is a creative artist who designed the blending hues of the rainbow and the intricacies of a butterfly's wings and the remarkable form of the newborn baby who nestles in its mother's arms.

In the same way, because our Creator is the perfect mathematician and physicist and biologist, we can now use nanotechnology to witness the tiny internal processes and biological machines that help our bodies run at the most microscopic of levels. From infinitesimal particles to the vastness of the universe, creation proclaims the glory of God.

The purpose of creation, however, goes beyond being an expression of God's magnificent talents. God also wanted to demonstrate His character in real and practical ways. To understand this, we need to back up to the most macro of levels. It is from this viewpoint that we can see God's hand in action.

In the history of the world, from the creation of heaven and earth to the re-creation of the new heavens and the new earth, there are four primary players. First is Israel. Second is the church. Third is the unbelieving world. There is also a fourth player—celestial beings. However, that fourth category isn't important for our current discussion. Between the first three there is constant interaction, beginning with Israel and the unbelieving world, and with the church now in the mix since the Day of Pentecost.

Most of Israel is currently part of the unbelieving world and will suffer the consequences of not following Christ. However, the people of Israel can also become part of the church through faith in Yeshua. I am an example of this, as are all the apostles and much of the earliest church. Paul was quick to remind the Philippians of his pedigree, saying, "If anyone else thinks he may have confidence in the flesh, I more so: circumcised the eighth day, of the stock of Israel, of the tribe of Benjamin, a Hebrew of the Hebrews; concerning the law, a Pharisee; concerning zeal, persecuting the church; concerning the righteousness which is in the law, blameless" (Philippians 3:4-6). While Paul ceased the persecutive activities he mentioned at the end of his mini-tirade, he never disavowed the ancestry he celebrated at the beginning.

As for the church, it is locked in its place. As much as some desire it, the church cannot become Israel. The people of Israel are an ethnic body chosen by God for a particular purpose, and He doesn't need a bunch of *goyim* crossing lines and muddying up His categories. In the same way, those in the church cannot become part of the unbelieving world. When you are saved, you become part of God's family and are adopted into the church through the Holy Spirit. Eternal life begins at that moment and cannot be taken away. Paul put it like this:

> Who shall separate us from the love of Christ? Shall tribulation, or distress, or persecution, or famine, or nakedness, or peril, or sword? As it is written: "For Your sake we are killed all day long; we are accounted as sheep for the slaughter." Yet in all these things we are more than conquerors through Him who loved us. For I am persuaded that neither death nor life, nor angels nor principalities nor powers, nor things present nor things to come, nor height nor depth, nor any other created thing, shall be able to separate us from the love of God which is in Christ Jesus our Lord (Romans 8:35-39).

What is missing from that list? Nothing. It is all-inclusive. The salvation Christ's death on the cross gives to us is not like an underage driver's permit. It's not a temporary card that you stick in your wallet as a hopeful placeholder for future permanency. There are some who think that as long as you don't get any tickets or hit any other cars or participate in any street takeovers, you'll eventually get your full-blown salvation license. That's not how it works.

There is no such thing as temporary eternal life. Like pregnancy, you are either saved or you are not. And when you receive Jesus as your Savior and Lord, you are absolutely, 100 percent saved. John made this crystal clear when he wrote, "This is the testimony: that God has given us eternal life, and this life is in

His Son. He who has the Son has life; he who does not have the Son of God does not have life" (1 John 5:11-12).

Again, don't be confused. Israel can be either unspiritual or spiritual, a concept we'll deal with more in the next chapter. By definition, however, the church is only spiritual. When unbelieving people, Jews or Gentiles, receive Yeshua as their Savior and Lord, the spiritually dead part of them is suddenly animated. It is born to life. Thus, while all are born physically, only Jews and Gentiles who give themselves to the Messiah receive this second birth. They are born again spiritually.

The church is the spiritual collection point of all these born-again people, both Jew and Gentile. Physical Israel is not the collection point—otherwise, Jews would just be staying put. Bodily, Jews and Gentiles always remain Jews and Gentiles, but spiritually, they can be united into God's family—the church. And by "the church," I am not referring to a denomination or a religion or a people group. I am speaking only of those who have followed through with Paul's mandate that "if you confess with your mouth that Jesus is Lord and believe in your heart that God raised him from the dead, you will be saved. For with the heart one believes and is justified, and with the mouth one confesses and is saved" (Romans 10:9-10 ESV). The church is a spiritual organism that unites all spiritually alive beings so that "there is neither Jew nor Greek, there is neither slave nor free, there is neither male nor female; for you are all one in Christ Jesus. And if you are Christ's, then you are Abraham's seed, and heirs according to the promise" (Galatians 3:28-29).

All post-Pentecost believers are in the church, but some are also in Israel. "Pardon me, Amir, but are you just going to gloss over the fact that Paul said that all in the church are Abraham's seed and heirs?" Yes. For now. But I promise to come back to this in the next chapter, when it will better fit the literary flow.

So, just to clarify: You can have a Jew who is also an unbeliever but who, through faith, can become part of the church. In fact, any part of the unbelieving world, no matter their ethnicity, has the opportunity—through Jesus' sacrifice—to become part of the church. All who belong to the church were once part of the unbelieving world, and, of those, some were also part of Israel. A day is soon coming when God will remove the church from the earth, which will usher in a seven-year period during which God will punish the wickedness of the unbelieving world and discipline the surviving remnant of Israel. At the end of the seven years, Jesus will return with the church, bringing judgment against unbelievers. When that happens, the Jews will finally recognize Him as the Messiah they pierced, individually give their lives to Him, "and so all Israel will be saved" (Romans 11:26). Got it? Good!

In this beautifully perfect plan, we see the grace, mercy, justice, and love of God. It's like we are living in a universal-scale pageant specifically designed to show the nature of our Creator. How do we know the grace and mercy of the Lord? All of us in the church experienced these characteristics when our sins were forgiven, and we were adopted into His family. How do we understand that justice is part of God's character? We see the way He has dealt with the wicked over the years. We also recognize the eternal judgment that is awaiting those who reject the Savior. And how can we be sure that God's love for His people is eternal and never-ending no matter how far we stray? For that, we have Israel.

KEEPING THE REMNANT

At Mount Sinai, God made a covenant with Israel. Through Moses, He said to the people, "'Now therefore, if you will indeed obey My voice and keep My covenant, then you shall be a special treasure to Me above all people; for all the earth is Mine. And you shall be to Me a kingdom of priests and a holy nation.' These are the words which you shall speak to the children of Israel" (Exodus 19:5-6). The first thing that we need to notice is that there is nothing here that supersedes or counteracts the Israel Decree, or Abrahamic covenant, given back in Genesis 12:1-3. In this passage, God is warning the people of Israel about the consequences of not following Him. Yes, they will remain special because of their physical lineage, but spiritually, they will not qualify to be God's chosen kingdom of priests. The nation of Israel, as a whole, cannot serve as a holy nation that reflects the character of God.

But even as the Lord spiritually rejects the corporate nation because of its sin, there will always be descendants of Abraham who will be God's special people spiritually. Remember when Elijah had a showdown with 450 priests of Baal on Mount Carmel? By showing them up in a fire-from-heaven-calling contest, he proved who was serving the true God. When King Ahab got back to his palace after witnessing the event and the subsequent slaughter of all the priests of Baal, he reported everything to Queen Jezebel. When it came to the Baal fan club of Israel, Jezebel was a charter member. Furious at what Elijah had done, she swore to kill him. Word quickly got to the old prophet, and he took off as fast as he could.

After 40 days of fleeing, Elijah found himself at Mount Horeb, also known as Mount Sinai. Exhausted, he found a cave and hid inside. It was there that God met him. Wind, an earthquake, and fire all rattled the prophet inside his hideaway. But when he heard a still, small voice, Elijah went to the cave's entrance and looked out.

"What are you doing here, Elijah?" (1 Kings 19:13).

This was the opening that the desperate, frustrated prophet was waiting for. He blurted out, "I have been very zealous for the LORD God of hosts; because the children of Israel have forsaken Your covenant, torn down Your altars, and killed Your prophets with the sword. I alone am left; and they seek to take my life" (verse 14).

When it came to the spiritual life of Israel, Elijah thought he was a solo act. In his mind, everyone else had deserted the Lord. If Jezebel managed to carry out her threats against the prophet, the worship of the true God would become extinct in the northern kingdom. God responded by telling Elijah to go back home because He had work for him to do. Though the prophet thought that he was the last of his kind, the Lord assured him, "I have reserved seven thousand in Israel, all whose knees have not bowed to Baal, and every mouth that has not kissed him" (verse 18). In other words, "Elijah, you are very special, but you're not *that* special. I've got more of you around."

Although the remnant of God-followers was small, there was still a remnant. That's how God operates. Even when the nation departs from Him, He always keeps some close. When Isaiah spoke about the fall of Babylon, he prophesied this about the chief gods of the prevailing empire of the time:

Bel bows down, Nebo stoops;
their idols were on the beasts and on the cattle.

Your carriages were heavily loaded,
a burden to the weary beast.
They stoop, they bow down together;
they could not deliver the burden,
but have themselves gone into captivity
(Isaiah 46:1-2).

The Babylonian people would try to protect their gods from the coming destruction. They would put their carved images on carts, but the weight would prove too much for the animals pulling them. Eventually, the idols would be captured and taken into captivity. So much for the power of Bel and Nebo.

The Lord then picked up the narrative and said to the people of the coming exile:

Listen to Me, O house of Jacob,
and all the remnant of the house of Israel,
who have been upheld by Me from birth,
who have been carried from the womb:
Even to your old age, I am He,
and even to gray hairs I will carry you!
I have made, and I will bear;
even I will carry, and will deliver you (verses 3-4).

What a contrast! The people of Babylon would try to carry their helpless gods away. But when it came to the all-powerful God, He did the carrying. From birth they were in His arms, and they remained there through their old age. And who were these people He cared for so much? They were the remnant of the house of Israel. They were the Jews who stayed true to Him through the dark years of Kings Manasseh and Amon and Zedekiah. They were the ones, like Daniel, Shadrach, Meshach, and Abednego, who never turned away from the Lord, even when they were stolen away from their land and forced to serve the pagan King Nebuchadnezzar. At times the descendants of Abraham who followed the Lord were many, and at times they were few. But they were always there. The light of the lamp was never fully extinguished.

Why would God put up with so much idolatry and disrespect from His people? It's very simple: love. God chose to have a special, loving relationship with Abraham's descendants. A perfect love is not something that is bestowed willy-nilly. It also isn't given, then withdrawn. One of the great Hebrew words used of God's love for Israel is *chesed*, which speaks of mercy, endurance, and a no-matter-what kind of love. This word is repeated in every verse in the great Psalm 136:

> Give thanks to the LORD, for he is good,
>> for his steadfast love endures forever.
> Give thanks to the God of gods,
>> for his steadfast love endures forever.
> Give thanks to the Lord of lords,
>> for his steadfast love endures forever;
> to him who alone does great wonders,
>> for his steadfast love endures forever
> (verses 1-4 ESV).

The Psalm continues like that for 26 verses, with each one reminding the reader that God's *chesed* is a never-ending love. The Lord is passionate for His people.

Admittedly, it doesn't always feel that way. When Elijah had Jezebel's henchman chasing after him, he was probably wondering where God was. In the times of King Manasseh, when he "shed very much innocent blood, till he had filled Jerusalem from one end to another" (2 Kings 21:16), much of that blood was likely from those who refused to worship his many idols. But even in the difficult times, God promises us that He is there. In Isaiah, when Zion cried out that God had forgotten and forsaken her, He replied:

> Can a woman forget her nursing child,
>   that she should have no compassion on
>   the son of her womb?
> Even these may forget,
>   yet I will not forget you.
> Behold, I have engraved you on the palms
> of my hands;
>   your walls are continually before me
> (Isaiah 49:15-16 ESV).

For those of you blessed with children, think of when you first held your baby in your arms. Remember the depth of your love and your commitment to care for and protect that child with all you have. If your love for your child was so rich and deep, imagine the vastness of the *chesed* love that your God has for you.

"But, Amir, Israel forfeited that love! The people worshipped idols and turned their backs on God. Worst of all, they rejected and crucified the Messiah. They killed God Himself!"

First, while Israel certainly had a hand in sending Jesus to the cross, it was Rome who crucified Him. Second, don't worry—Yeshua didn't stay dead. Third, it was all part of the Father's plan from before creation, so the crucifixion was no surprise to anyone in the Godhead. And finally, is that really how little you think of God's love?

Imagine that the little baby you held in your hands is now a grown adult. But she's far from God. She's making wrong choice after wrong choice. She's hurt you, stolen from you, and cursed you to your face. Or maybe your son has become a violent man. He's beaten his wife and his kids. He's even knocked you down a time or two. Or is he a predator? Has he hurt women, the elderly, or children?

I know, those are horrible things to think about. But I have no doubt that some of you reading this book are in that very place. However, no matter what your child has done, they are still your child. Their words may break your heart, and their actions may take your breath away. Sadly, for some, the situation may be too much. Tragically, for your sake and especially for theirs, you may have disowned them, told them that you never want to have anything to do with them again.

But there are many others—a majority of others, I'd dare say—who do what they can to continue demonstrating their love to their children no matter what they do. That love may take different shapes and forms at times. Sometimes love may mean separating yourself from them for a season until they hit rock bottom. It may mean turning a son or daughter over to authorities so that victims are protected and justice is served. But even amid those actions, your love never wanes. It may be tested, but it never ceases. If human love can be that steadfast, that unceasing, that longsuffering, how can we ever claim that God's is less so?

ALL LAW AND NO HEART

God's relationship with Israel has always been a rocky one. There have been times of close ties, like during the reigns of David, Hezekiah, Josiah, and other good kings. But even then, there was always an underbelly of rebellion within the kingdom. When Saul was king and his jealousy of David was at a high, he plotted to kill his loyal servant in the young warrior's home. David's wife and Saul's daughter, Michal, caught wind of his plan. She rushed to her husband and told him, "If you do not save your life tonight, tomorrow you will be killed" (1 Samuel 19:11).

David escaped through a window, and Michal took one of the household idols and set it in the bed, putting goat's hair on it to disguise the head. Saul's guards came to watch the condemned man so that he could then be taken to Saul in the morning to be killed. But Michal hustled them away, showing them the fake David and telling them that he was sick. When the guards returned to Saul, he was indignant, demanding they bring David to him on his sickbed so that he could do away with him once and for all. When the guards returned, the ruse was discovered.

What strikes me most about this account is not Saul's hatred for David or Michal's complicity in a conspiracy to trick her own father. It's the ready accessibility of a household idol to put in the bed. What in the world was it doing there to begin with?

Idolatry was the go-to belief system of civilization at that time, and the Hebrews were not immune to its trappings. When they were in Egypt, many of them fell into the allure of their masters' pagan gods and worshipped their idols. When God gave instructions for Moses to relay to the people about proper sacrifices, He concluded, "They shall no more offer their sacrifices to demons, after whom they have played the harlot. This shall be a statute forever for them throughout their generations" (Leviticus 17:7). Tough words, but rather than focusing on the big *h* word that describes their actions, I think there are two other words that are of even greater importance—"no more." Those words call for the cessation of an action that has been taking place and continues to take place.

Sadly, God's call for "no more" was never fully obeyed. Or, if it was, it was only for brief times. The book of Judges describes continual and repeated downward cycles of the people worshipping foreign gods, God bringing enemies to teach Israel a lesson through suppression, the Israelites realizing their sin and crying out to God for help, God rescuing them, then their falling back into the worship of foreign gods again. Over and over. Lather, rinse, repeat.

The same cycles happened under the kings. Even during the reigns of some of the good kings in the south, the high places for worship weren't removed, and in many households, the idols remained. God finally got so fed up that He sent the people into exile so that He could purge the evil from the nation and the land itself could experience its neglected Sabbath rests. When the Israelites came back after the exile, they were committed to following God. At least for a while.

What emerged in post-exilic Israel was a new brand of idolatry, the worship of the law. It had its roots in the code given to Moses, but the religious leaders of the time were so paranoid that they might fall once again into idol worship that they heaved the pendulum the other direction with all their might. They created a man-made law to surround and protect the God-given law—a 1,000-foot-high impenetrable barrier set far enough back from the actual law that no one would ever risk breaking it. It was a legal buffer zone of massive proportions, designed to protect the purity of the nation.

But what they did to create this Kevlar law-coating was to suck the heart from the Torah so they could focus on the words themselves. They thought that as long as they followed the letters, they'd be safe. Forget mercy, forget compassion. They weren't interested in peace, love, and understanding. Their traditions said, "Do," so people did. Their traditions said, "Don't," so people didn't. No exceptions. No caveats.

These post-exilic priests and Pharisees weren't the first ones to try this mindless, soulless, AI form of legalism. It was this letter-of-the-law mindset that had God telling the Jews through the prophet Hosea, "I desire mercy and not sacrifice, and the knowledge of God more than burnt offerings" (6:6). And in Isaiah, God makes the accusation that the people "draw near with their mouths and honor Me with their lips, but have removed their hearts far from Me, and their fear toward Me is taught by the commandment of men" (29:13). There was no relationship between God and man, only God-attributed rules taught by one man to another. That was not what the Lord intended.

One other passage had a profound impact on my life. In the first chapter of Isaiah, the Lord was laying it hard on the people of Judah. He said:

> "To what purpose is the multitude of your sacrifices
> to Me?" says the LORD.

"I have had enough of burnt offerings of rams
  and the fat of fed cattle.
I do not delight in the blood of bulls,
  or of lambs or goats.

"When you come to appear before Me,
  who has required this from your hand,
  to trample My courts?
Bring no more futile sacrifices;
  incense is an abomination to Me.
The New Moons, the Sabbaths, and the calling
  of assemblies—
I cannot endure iniquity and the sacred meeting.
Your New Moons and your appointed feasts
  My soul hates;
They are a trouble to Me,
I am weary of bearing them" (Isaiah 1:11-14).

I remember, as a new believer, reading those words. They shook me to the core, to such an extent that I nearly lost my faith. How could this God of love and mercy suddenly sound so angry and hypocritical? "'To what purpose' You ask, Lord? How about because You said so! You set up the sacrificial system for Israel to follow, but now You are tearing the people apart for doing exactly what You demanded they do!"

How could a loving God be that capricious? How would I ever know whether obedience was what He wanted, or if by doing what He asked I'd be carrying out what His soul hates? It was only after much prayer and wise counsel that I came to learn that the people were following the rules but without heart, exactly what Isaiah opined later in chapter 6, and Hosea wrote about in his book. God wanted compassion. He wanted mercy. He wanted the heart. Once He had the heart, following the rules would be the natural product.

Israel didn't get that. Yet despite all these misunderstandings of God's intent, misapplications of His law, and outright rebellion by the people, the Lord never stopped loving Israel. Once again, think of this in terms of God's desire to not only tell the world about His love through His great book, but to practically demonstrate His never-failing *chesed* through His relationship with the Jewish people.

DISCIPLINE ENDS, LOVE DOESN'T

Hosea had it bad as a prophet. Being one of God's chosen messengers was not a cushy job by any stretch of the imagination because the Lord tended toward using their lives as practical, and often harsh, examples. As real-life experiences went, I would put Hosea one step better than Isaiah walking around naked for three years (Isaiah 20:1-4) and one step worse than Ezekiel losing his beloved wife overnight (Ezekiel 24:15-18).

When the Lord called Hosea to be a prophet, He went all in. There was no gradual easing him into the role.

When the Lord began to speak by Hosea, the Lord said to Hosea:

"Go, take yourself a wife of harlotry
and children of harlotry,

> for the land has committed great harlotry
> by departing from the LORD."

So he went and took Gomer the daughter of Diblaim,
and she conceived and bore him a son (Hosea 1:2-3).

Strong words for a painful task. You've got to think his mind was asking, *Yikes! Any chance I could just spend three days in the belly of a great fish?* But like Abraham, who followed each of God's calls to action with an equal and appropriate reaction, Hosea immediately obeyed. He married the lovely Gomer and the two set about starting a family. The first child, a son, was given by God the name Jezreel to indicate the why and the where of the impending destruction of the northern kingdom of Israel. All I need to do is look out the back window of my house to see the valley that bears this child's name.

The second child, a girl, was given the tragic name of Lo-Ruhamah, which means "no mercy," or "not loved." Between her name and her family situation, I'm guessing this poor girl had some challenges to overcome. But there was a purpose to young Lo-Ruhamah's name. She was a declaration to the northern kingdom that God was done with them. They had gone too far, and now they were on their own. But she was also an encouragement to the southern kingdom of Judah that God hadn't yet given up on them and He would miraculously save them from the Assyrian juggernaut that was about to swallow up their northern brothers.

A third child came, another boy, and he was given the name Lo-Ammi, meaning "not my people." Not a great name for a kid, but still better than Lo-Ruhamah. He was one more reminder to the people of Israel in the north that they were no longer God's children. He was done. They'd gone too far.

"Hold on a second, Amir. You were saying that God never gave up on Israel. Now you just told us that Lo-Ruhamah and Lo-Ammi were living, toddling proof that He actually was done with them." I hear what you're saying, and I understand your conclusions. But, as I often say, if you want to truly understand the Bible, you need to keep reading. Context, context, context. If you keep forging through this sad family origin story, you'll see God give a promise:

> Yet the number of the children of Israel
> shall be as the sand of the sea,
> which cannot be measured or numbered.
> And it shall come to pass
> in the place where it was said to them,
> "You are not My people,"
> there it shall be said to them,
> "You are sons of the living God."
> Then the children of Judah and the children of Israel
> shall be gathered together,
> and appoint for themselves one head;
> and they shall come up out of the land,
> for great will be the day of Jezreel!
> Say to your brethren, "My people,"
> and to your sisters, "Mercy is shown" (1:10–2:1).

Context is everything. God was fed up with *those* people. But He still had a commitment to *the* people. That generation of individuals from the northern kingdom experienced the just punishment for their sin and rebellion. But "they" isn't inclusive of "them." God did not throw Hosea's symbolically named babies out with the bathwater. His perfect love, demonstrated by His commitment to the Jewish people, is too great for that. Unfortunately for Hosea, he was about to be pushed a step further so that he could become the perfect example of God's unfailing love.

Married life was not for Gomer. There were too many places to go, too many people to see, too many guys to…well…meet. When she couldn't take it any longer, she was out the door. Who knows whether this was a relief to Hosea or not? He very well may have breathed a sigh of relief and thought, *Well, that's over and done with. It certainly can't get any worse.* Time passed, and then suddenly, things got worse.

> Then the LORD said to me, "Go again, love a woman who is loved by a lover and is committing adultery, just like the love of the LORD for the children of Israel, who look to other gods and love the raisin cakes of the pagans."
>
> So I bought her for myself for fifteen shekels of silver, and one and one-half homers of barley. And I said to her, "You shall stay with me many days; you shall not play the harlot, nor shall you have a man—so, too, will I be toward you."
>
> For the children of Israel shall abide many days without king or prince, without sacrifice or sacred pillar, without ephod or teraphim. Afterward the

children of Israel shall return and seek the LORD their
God and David their king. They shall fear the LORD
and His goodness in the latter days (3:1-5).

First, notice the words "just like the love of the LORD for the
children of Israel." God wasn't asking Hosea to do anything that
He hadn't had to do Himself over and over with His chosen people. Both the northern kingdom of Israel and the southern kingdom of Judah had repeatedly prostituted themselves. But, still,
God's love never ran out. And it never will.

How do I know that God's love will remain? Look at the last
two sentences. The children of Israel will return to God and seek
to be ruled by the line of David. They will be the nation that He
had first intended them to be way back when the Israel Decree
was first given, living up to the one standard they had never been
able to fulfill—being a witness of God to the nations.

There are those who will link this to Peter's first epistle, and
rightfully so. It's impossible to miss the connections:

> You are a chosen generation, a royal priesthood, a
> holy nation, His own special people, that you may
> proclaim the praises of Him who called you out of
> darkness into His marvelous light; who once were not
> a people but are now the people of God, who had
> not obtained mercy but now have obtained mercy
> (1 Peter 2:9-10).

Before salvation, those who make up the church were a bunch
of random people from different nations and various backgrounds.

But God has united all believers into one body for the purpose of showing His light to the world. At one time, we were all random folk, "Lo-Ammi." But now we are a people. Formerly, we were dead in our sins, separated from the mercy of God. But now He has taken "Lo-Ruhamah" and transformed us into individuals who have received His life-changing mercy. Undoubtedly, Peter had this very passage from Hosea in mind when he was writing his epistle.

But it is an illogical leap to suddenly say that the latter has superseded the position of the former, that the church has now stepped into the place of Israel. There is nothing in either Hosea's or Peter's words that indicates any substitution has taken place. This is not an either/or situation. Israel forfeited its calling to be God's witnesses to the world, but the Lord's love and mercy will one day restore the Jewish people into that role. In the meantime, He has given the job to the church, who were not a people before they received God's mercy, but now together form one family.

As we said before, God is telling His story, revealing Himself, and He is doing it through Israel, the church, and the unbelieving world. We put unnecessary and inappropriate restrictions on Him when we say He can work through only one group at a time. It's His story. Let Him tell it His way.

One final question: Has this restoration of Israel predicted in Hosea 3 happened yet? Not that I've seen, and I've been looking pretty hard in my home country. It wasn't true of post-exilic, legalistic Israel, and it certainly isn't true of secular, hedonistic Israel today. Could we have missed it? Might Israel's restoration have been a brief blip, here today and gone the next? Could Zerubbabel's first group or maybe the nation under Ezra or Nehemiah

have lived this blip long enough to meet the minimal propheti-
cal requirements for fulfillment?

Hosea's words tell us no. But he also assures us that we need
not worry. This final "come to Yeshua" moment will not come
until "the latter days" (Hosea 3:5). What will that look like? We
already know. We've talked about it. When the Lord returns with
His church to the Mount of Olives at the end of the tribulation,
the people of Israel will recognize the Messiah they rejected. They
will fear the Lord and be awed at His goodness and unfailing love.
Falling to their knees, they will repent of their sin and rebellion,
and "so all Israel will be saved" (Romans 11:26).

What an amazing sight that will be!

CHAPTER 4

YOU CAN'T
UN-ISRAEL ISRAEL

The Lord has blessed me with an amazing wife, and together we have four children—three sons and a daughter. My oldest son loves the Lord and by his life sets an example for his younger siblings. This is not unusual for a firstborn. They typically take on that role as leader of the kids. But my daughter, second in birth order, is also very strong in her own right. In fact, after the horrible events of October 7, she was the first in our family to volunteer in her reserve unit back into active duty. Eventually, both her older brother and the one just behind her also served. Our youngest is not yet old enough. All our children are remarkable and are gifted in their own ways. It is our similarities as well as our differences that make us a family.

Why did God need both Israel and the church? Couldn't He have gotten by with just one or the other? Of course He could have. He's God. But as He laid out the plan that would best show His character to the world, He determined that two are better than one in His family. Remember, He gave Israel at least three ways to bless the nations. Give the world His Word—check. Give the world the Savior—check. Be God's witness to humanity—*oy*, not so much. That's why it was so great that there was a younger brother to come along and pick up the slack. How wonderful it was that the church could step into the role of salt and light, spreading the truth to the nations.

But the church's mission is not only to the world at large. It is also specifically to its older brother, Israel. Israel has religion. The church has relationship. Israel has law. The church has love. It's as if the people of Israel are now standing outside of Eden, talking and dreaming about what it must be like inside as they voice ritual prayers to the God who lives past the flaming swords of the guardian cherubim. The church, meanwhile, is inside the garden, worshipping in the Lord's presence and fellowshipping with Him face to face. The plan, as God laid it out, is for Israel on the outside to be provoked to jealousy (Romans 11:11) by those on the inside as they listen to all the joy and celebration and whooping it up that is taking place. What they'll find one day is that when they approach the guardian cherubim through faith in Yeshua, whom they had previously rejected, the flaming swords will separate, and they'll be able to enter directly into the presence of God.

What a beautiful plan! Far too intricate for an either/or, but perfectly suited for God's both/and.

IS NOT ALL ISRAEL
REALLY NOT ALL ISRAEL?

Thus far in this book, we've seen the legal basis for the existence of the State of Israel. We've also looked at the origins of this chosen nation and the promise of its unending nature. In the most recent chapter, we saw how God's covenant decree is greater by far than any human rebellion or sin. Individual iniquity will lead people to eternal separation from God, but it is not enough to negate a greater nationwide commitment made by the Lord no matter how high the percentage is of rebelling individuals. In other words, human sin cannot negate God's corporate promise.

Going back to our football analogy, our team defense has been established and backed up by Scripture. The people of modern Israel are the beloved nation of Abraham's physical line. If they were not, then for the church, what's happening in Israel is no different than the Russia/Ukraine war or the cross-border battles the Kurds are having with Iran, Turkey, and others. But because they are God's chosen people, the church has an obligation to care for and pray for the nation.

With that firm foundation laid, we can now go on the offense and deal with some of the primary biblical passages used by Reformed theologians to support their belief that, whether by original plan or Israel's sinful forfeiture, the church has superseded Israel as God's chosen people.

At first pass, Romans 2:28-29 can present a thorny problem. Paul wrote:

> He is not a Jew who is one outwardly, nor is circumcision that which is outward in the flesh; but he is a Jew who is one inwardly; and circumcision is that of the heart, in the Spirit, not in the letter; whose praise is not from men but from God.

Ouch! To some, this says that you Jews out there who think you are really Jews—you're not! You may have been in the past, but there is now a new covenant. Physical doesn't matter anymore. That's old covenant. What matters now is spiritual. So forget your pedigree and look at your heart. If you have been sealed by the Holy Spirit through salvation, only then can you be a true Jew, even if you happen to be a Gentile.

Before I answer this, I might as well throw in one more passage from Romans, because these two appear to be saying the same thing:

> They are not all Israel who are of Israel, nor are they all children because they are the seed of Abraham; but, "In Isaac your seed shall be called." That is, those who are the children of the flesh, these are not the children of God; but the children of the promise are counted as the seed (9:6-8).

Again, Paul seems to be saying to quit putting your faith in your flesh. Just because you were born of Israel doesn't mean you really are of Israel—at least, not in the way that really matters. The people of physical Israel are not really the children of God. That appellation belongs to the children of promise. Where are these children of promise currently found? In the church.

The problem with the replacement interpretation of these passages is in the underlying presupposition that forces replacement proponents to see Paul's statements as words of negation rather than addition. "If you are not the spiritual children of God, then you cannot be children of God at all. Why? Because there can be only one set of God's children." To that I will respond with the same question: Why? Where does Scripture say that God must discard the first in order to accept the second? Why can't God still have a special plan for the physical line of Abraham while carrying out His plan for a spiritual line of Abraham?

The only way to make these passages fit a replacement doctrine is to go in with the presupposition that it is okay to redefine word meanings. Or, even more so, to say that Paul intended the reader to redefine word meanings. "I'm going to use the word *Israel* here, figuring that readers will have figured out by now that I really mean *the church*. I mean, I've hinted at it enough already, haven't I?" But if you look at the nearly 80 times that "Israel" is used in the New Testament, not once does it refer to anyone who is not ethnically Jewish. Even in Romans 2, to whom is Paul speaking?

> Indeed you are called a Jew, and rest on the law, and make your boast in God, and know His will, and approve the things that are excellent, being instructed out of the law, and are confident that you yourself are a guide to the blind, a light to those who are in darkness, an instructor of the foolish, a teacher of babes, having the form of knowledge and truth in the law (verses 17-20).

Paul's words are to Israel, and he is challenging the people to not simply rest on the law and on their heritage for salvation. God has given a different way, the way of Yeshua, whose gospel is the power of God to salvation for every believing person, "for the Jew first and also for the Greek" (1:16). In the flesh, these two ethnic groups remain separate parts of God's great pageant for showing His character to the world. It is only in the spiritual realm, in Christ Jesus, that we are united as spiritual children. In Him,

> there is neither Jew nor Greek, there is neither slave nor free, there is neither male nor female; for you are all one in Christ Jesus. And if you are Christ's, then you are Abraham's seed, and heirs according to the promise (Galatians 3:28-29).

In the body of Christ, the Jew and Greek become one. Together, we are the spiritual seed of Abraham. But that doesn't mean there is no longer a distinction between us. In Paul's time, there were some believers who were slaves and some who were free—a clear distinction. Believe it or not, male and female will always remain different genders, no matter what the therapists counsel or how many hormones you pump into your body. So why is it only when it comes to ethnicity that the replacement folk say the differences go out the window?

A Jew will always be a Jew, and a Gentile will always be a Gentile. Physically, they begin in two different categories, but spiritually, they enter the world in the same lost state. "There is none righteous, no, not one" (Romans 3:10). When it comes to the flesh, neither will ever move from one category to the other. Jews, as a people, will always be the physical chosen of God, and Gentiles will not. But when it comes to the spiritual, both have the exact same opportunity to move from unsaved to saved through the exact same methodology. "For the wages of sin is death, but the gift of God is eternal life in Christ Jesus our Lord" (6:23).

The only advantage the Jews ever received when it comes to

salvation is that when the truth came, it did so to them first. But when Jesus was rejected by the spiritual leadership of Israel, the gospel was given to the Gentiles. A day is soon coming when once again, Christ will reveal Himself to the nation of Israel, and in that blessed day, the Jewish people will finally be ready to accept Him as their promised Messiah.

IS GOD TAKING THE KINGDOM FROM ISRAEL AND GIVING IT TO ANOTHER?

Another passage used by the replacement theologians is spoken by Jesus during the final week before His crucifixion. The Lord is at the temple and is having it out with the chief priests and Pharisees. He's denied their request to verify His authority for His teaching. He's told two parables—one about two sons, and one about a landowner—both ripping the spiritual leaders apart for their unbelief and their rejection of God's prophets. Building to a finale, He says, "Therefore I say to you, the kingdom of God will be taken from you and given to a nation bearing the fruits of it" (Matthew 21:43). The kingdom of God taken away and given to another? That is about as harsh as it comes.

To understand what Jesus is saying, we need to answer two questions. First, what is this kingdom of God? Second, to whom is He addressing this? When we look at the phrase "kingdom of God," let's start with what He is not saying. There is no mention of the land. There is no mention of a relationship with the Father. In fact, nowhere in this passage do we see at all the Israel Decree given to Abraham, except when it comes to a single portion of the blessing.

Remember, the blessing came in three parts. There was the Word of God. Obviously, Jesus wasn't talking about that because the New Testament was still to be written by Jewish hands. There was the giving of the Messiah. That one could be emphatically checked off the list as perfectly accomplished. That left the testimony of God and His salvation to the world. This, Israel had botched so badly that nobody with any true perspective could argue that they had not forfeited their opportunity.

What's being talked about here as the kingdom of God is the spiritual relationship with the Lord that comes through Yeshua. Israel wasn't living it, and certainly wasn't showing it, so God was going to pass that off to a new entity—the church. Nothing is said here by Jesus about any other facet of the Father's relationship with Israel. They are still as much His physical children as they've ever been. Unfortunately, their rebellion through idolatry of the law led them to a place where they were going to have to face some seriously tough love to bring them to a readiness for repentance. That is what the tribulation, made Israel-centric by the phrase "the time of Jacob's trouble" (Jeremiah 30:7), is all about.

The second question we need to ask is, To whom is Jesus speaking? Again, it's all about context. Jesus began chapter 21 talking to the chief priests and Pharisees, and at the end of the chapter, we can see that they were still His audience. Matthew wrote, "Now when the chief priests and Pharisees heard His parables, they perceived that He was speaking of them" (21:45). The rebuke that Jesus gave was directed specifically at the religious leaders. Why was He going after them? Because they were terrible shepherds. They were leading the people away from God rather than toward

Him. They were spiritual pied pipers, but they were marching the people toward the merciless idolatry of legalism.

In one of Jesus' angry tirades against the spiritual leaders and the experts of the Torah law, He accused them, saying, "Woe to you also, lawyers! For you load men with burdens hard to bear, and you yourselves do not touch the burdens with one of your fingers...You have taken away the key of knowledge. You did not enter in yourselves, and those who were entering in you hindered" (Luke 11:46, 52). They weighed people down with dos and don'ts, and when the weight became too much, they simply watched them collapse. The spiritual leaders had full access to the path that would lead the people of Israel to the lush green pastures of truth, but they neglected their obligation. Instead of working hard for the sake of the sheep, they basked in the trappings of the population's glory and honor and admiration.

Sadly, this was nothing new for Israel's spiritual leaders. Through Jeremiah, the Lord condemned the spiritual shepherds of Israel:

> "Woe to the shepherds who destroy and scatter the sheep of My pasture!" says the Lord. Therefore thus says the Lord God of Israel against the shepherds who feed My people: "You have scattered My flock, driven them away, and not attended to them. Behold, I will attend to you for the evil of your doings," says the Lord. "But I will gather the remnant of My flock out of all countries where I have driven them, and bring them back to their folds; and they shall be fruitful and increase. I will set up shepherds over them who will feed them; and they shall fear no more, nor be

dismayed, nor shall they be lacking," says the LORD
(Jeremiah 23:1-4).

The shepherds neglected their responsibilities, and the people
bought into their lies. Therefore, the nation as a whole would
pay a price. But notice that even though God condemned the
shepherds, He left the people with a promise. After their time
of discipline was done, He would bring a remnant back to the
land of Israel. There, they would be under true shepherds who
would feed them the spiritual food they were lacking. Doesn't
that sound exactly like what we've been saying about God's plan
for Israel in the tribulation?

We see the same story play out in Ezekiel 34. The shepherds
refused to properly lead the sheep, so the sheep were scattered.
God stepped in, saying, "Behold, I am against the shepherds,
and I will require My flock at their hand" (verse 10). The Lord
will step in as the shepherd and will bring the flock back to the
high mountains of Israel. He promised, "I will feed them in good
pasture, and their fold shall be on the high mountains of Israel.
There they shall lie down in a good fold and feed in rich pasture
on the mountains of Israel" (verse 14).

In Jeremiah and Ezekiel, as well as in Jesus' rebuke in Matthew,
the targets are the spiritual leaders of Israel who are neglecting
their role as shepherds. They are the ones whom God is rejecting. The sheep are still responsible for their own sins, and as a
result, they are scattered in punishment. But at no time does
the Lord permanently turn His back on them. They are still His
flock. The remnant remains.

In today's world, we see a time when Israel has been brought back to the land according to the promise of Ezekiel. Sure, the people had returned after the exile, but the godly spiritual leadership they had didn't last long. And if you continue to read Ezekiel 34, you'll see that there is a coming time of peace in the land as has never been seen. It is not only a peace that exists with other nations, but between humanity and nature. There is not enough space here for me to go into all that is described in the last 12 verses of the chapter, but if you read them, you will know that the words contain a wonderful promise that can be fulfilled only when the Savior is reigning from His throne in Jerusalem.

ARE ONLY THOSE OF
FAITH SONS OF ABRAHAM?

Our next controversial passage is found in Galatians 3. In the letter to the Galatian church, Paul comes out hot. He had thought all was going well there, but then rumors reached him that some Judaizers had invaded the premises. These legalistic Jewish leaders came saying, "Hey, faith is great and all, but you also have to follow the Torah." The Gentiles in the Galatian church began to get confused. After all, these were fancily dressed Jews who were using high-falutin' words to chastise their lack of law. Christianity began with the Jews, so who were they as Gentiles to question what these guys said? Besides, all those rules and feasts and other things sure sounded important. Maybe the new spiritual sheriffs in town were right, and Paul had accidentally forgotten to mention the law part to them.

Paul wasted no time in shutting that down:

> I marvel that you are turning away so soon from Him
> who called you in the grace of Christ, to a different
> gospel, which is not another; but there are some who
> trouble you and want to pervert the gospel of Christ.
> But even if we, or an angel from heaven, preach any
> other gospel to you than what we have preached to
> you, let him be accursed. As we have said before, so
> now I say again, if anyone preaches any other gospel to
> you than what you have received, let him be accursed
> (Galatians 1:6-9).

The apostle then pivots to giving his spiritual pedigree, describing his early years as part of the church. Eventually, he gets to his great culminating statement, saying, "I have been crucified with Christ; it is no longer I who live, but Christ lives in me; and the life which I now live in the flesh I live by faith in the Son of God, who loved me and gave Himself for me. I do not set aside the grace of God; for if righteousness comes through the law, then Christ died in vain" (2:20-21). It is grace, not law, that saves!

But Paul is not done. He's still fuming, as is evidenced by his next line: "O foolish Galatians!" (3:1). He tells them to think back to their own salvation. Was it by law or by grace? Or, if you want to go back even further, let's go all the way to the receiver of the Israel Decree. Was Abraham justified by the law? Of course not! He didn't even have the law, you moops! Paul wrote, "Abraham 'believed God, and it was accounted to him for righteousness'" (3:6)!

Now we come to the kicker verse: "Therefore know that only those who are of faith are sons of Abraham" (verse 7). I've got a feeling that you can write the rest of this paragraph because we're building on a theme. But I'll type this out anyway, because I want it to become second nature to you. Abraham was promised land, seed, and blessing. The land is Israel, and the seed is the Jews. The blessing breaks into how many parts? Three. Abraham's descendants will be a blessing through the Word of God, the Messiah, and their spiritual testimony. Except they weren't a blessing, at least as far as part three.

The people of Israel were given one opportunity after another to get their spiritual walk right, but other than at brief moments now and then, they never could fully live the truth of God before the nations. So God took that single spiritual part of the blessing from them and gave it to the church. What happened to the rest of the Abrahamic covenant? Jesus never stopped being a physical Jew. The physical Bible was not replaced by a new Gentile version. Those two parts of the blessing continued onward solid and intact. Why would we now say that the promise of the physical seed no longer matters, and the guarantee of the physical land is now moot?

Or are we saying that all three parts of the Abrahamic covenant, including the seed and the land, have passed on to the church? The only way we can do that is by making everything spiritual. And the only way to do that is by allegorizing the words of the Abrahamic covenant. God's promise of physical land to Israel was a picture of a greater promise of spiritual land for the church, a new heavens and new earth. God's promise of physical seed realized by the nation of Israel is now superseded by the true spiritual seed—a new people, a holy nation—made up of Abraham's true children of faith found only in the church.

But why would we do that? What is the compulsion that forces some to give this simple, literal promise given to Abraham such a forced, complicated meaning? We already saw the answer to that earlier in the words and attitudes of the church fathers, who were determined to cut "Christ-killing Israel" out of God's plan no matter what it took.

It is solely in the spiritual realm relating to salvation that it makes sense to christen all people of faith as sons of Abraham. Outside of that one lane, nothing else can be touched logically or biblically. Why is there no great rush of new Gentile believers moving to Israel? Because it's not their land. There's no pull. But there is a great flood of Jewish unbelievers who are making aliyah to the Promised Land. They don't have God, but still they go, because deep in their being they feel the call. As we saw in Ezekiel, God said He would lead His people back. That movement is taking place as you read these words.

WHAT IS THE ISRAEL OF GOD?

For the next difficult verse, we've got to go almost to the end of the letter to the Galatians. Paul was saying his farewells and getting in a few final reminders that it's grace, not law, that saves. He wrote, "In Christ Jesus neither circumcision nor uncircumcision avails anything, but a new creation" (6:15). Good so far. It's not law or anything done in the flesh that matters, but a new person created in Christ Jesus. But then he adds, "As many as walk according to this rule, peace and mercy be upon them, and upon the Israel of God" (verse 16). Hmmm…Israel of God? What is that?

There are two concerns with that last phrase. One is that the wording is unusual. In fact, it is the only place in the Bible that you'll read it. This has led some to believe that it is referring to something special, something unique. If Paul had meant plain old Israel, he would have simply written "Israel." Therefore, he was probably trying to communicate something new here. And, if you have a presupposition toward the replacement camp, it is possible to look at the context of the entire letter to the Galatians and say, "Paul is obviously making a distinction here between the Israel of the old covenant and the Israel of the new covenant, known as the church, which he here calls the Israel of God."

Not convinced yet? There is one more small piece of evidence that can have a major impact on how we understand this. The full last phrase reads "and upon the Israel of God." The word "and," in the original Greek text, is *kai*. Typically, *kai* is a connecting conjunction. However, it can also be translated as "also, even, too, so." That is why in some translations, you'll find the end of this verse saying "peace and mercy be upon them, which are the Israel of God." This translative interpretation takes all believers and forms them into one group, labeling them as "the Israel of God."

Is it really possible to read the Greek text this way? By all means! But it is not the typical reading, nor is it the one adopted by most modern translations. It is true that the New Testament is filled with passages that rightfully adopt a secondary reading to *kai* and many other Greek words. But when that is done, there always has to be a justifiable reason. In this case, the most obvious reason to not go with the primary reading of "and" is a bias toward replacement theology. But is that reason enough?

Typically, when Paul writes a letter, he begins with a theology section. Then once he's finished explaining the doctrine, he moves on to how you should then live. One of the clearest examples of this is the letter to the Romans. In the first 11 chapters, Paul gives deep theology. Then when he opens chapter 12, he does so with the word "therefore." In other words, he's given the *what*, and now he's moving to four concluding chapters of *so what?*, or *how do I live out what I've just read?*, before closing with a final chapter of greetings.

This is the pattern we find in Galatians. Paul began with four chapters of theology. Then, what do you find in the first verse of chapter 5? "Therefore." He launches his *so what?* section talking about standing firm in the freedom of Christ, then moves on to walking in the Spirit, what the fruit of the Spirit looks like, and how to properly show love to one another.

Finally, Paul gets to his conclusion. He is winding down. This isn't the time for controversy. This isn't the time to shake things up. He reminds the Christians in Galatia of his main point to not give in to the Judaizing, legalistic crowd. He assures them that he will never boast of anything except the grace he's received through the cross of Christ. Then he wishes peace and mercy upon all who put their hope in God's grace and not in the law, both to those who are believing Gentiles and to those who are believing Jews—the Israel of God. It's really a very simple literal read. Sometimes the word "and" simply means "and." This is one of those times.

ARE THE JEWS REALLY
THE SYNAGOGUE OF SATAN?

The last two passages we're going to look at are big ones. They are the flagship verses of the antisemites. It seems that every time I post something online about supporting Israel or praying for the nation, people pop out of whatever hidey-hole they've been in so they can write to me. I don't know if they've ever read the book of Revelation or if they know the Scriptures at all. What I am sure of is that they have these two verses memorized to perfection. They are Revelation 2:9 and 3:9. They whip them out and wield them like swords, believing that with these two weapons they'll be able to cut the legs out from under any pro-Israel argument.

In the first passage, Jesus was speaking to the church in Smyrna. The message He was about to give them was one of encouragement under persecution and hope for when the trial had passed. After His introduction, the Lord dictated to John, "I know your works, tribulation, and poverty (but you are rich); and I know the blasphemy of those who say they are Jews and are not, but are a synagogue of Satan" (Revelation 2:9). Oof—"synagogue of Satan"! Harsh words!

The second of the two troubling sentences is found in Jesus' words to the church in Philadelphia. This congregation was a gold-star church, and they were about to hear words from the Lord that would make their hearts soar. As He was affirming them for their steadfastness, He included the statement, "Indeed I will make those of the synagogue of Satan, who say they are Jews and are not, but lie—indeed I will make them come and worship before your feet, and to know that I have loved you" (3:9). There it is again—the "synagogue of Satan." Made up of who? People who say they're Jews, but really are not. Undoubtedly, Jesus is speaking of the Jewish people who still lay claim to all the promises given to Abraham, not realizing that they've been kicked to the curb by the Father for their unbelief. Right?

Let's look at two common interpretations.

First, there are those who say this synagogue of Satan was made up of men and women impersonating Jews. There was something about Judaism that attracted them, pulling them like a magnet. So they took on Jewish characteristics. They acted like Jews, maybe dressed like Jews, and did their best to follow the law and the feasts. Ultimately, however, their loyalty did not shift to God but remained with Caesar. So when they sought to integrate themselves into the church, they created havoc with their semi-paganish, somewhat Jewy, sort of Christian-like ways. So that's one option. I'm not saying it's a great one and its foundation is almost entirely speculation, but it's an interpretation that some folks hold to.

The second interpretation says these are Gentile believers who believe they are now Israel because the church replaced the nation. Sound a little familiar? Based on this understanding, it would mean that Jesus is looking at these people and saying, "What are you doing? The Father created certain roles for certain people so that He could show who He is, and you're muddling it all up. Stay in your Gentile lane!" The result of blurring these lines could wreak such major havoc on God's great plan that Jesus labels its origins as satanic.

Before we move on, let me make one thing clear. I'm not saying that those who teach or who believe in replacement theology are intentionally serving as servants of the enemy. I believe that it is entirely possible that people can spend their lives studying the Word of God, but because they are influenced by presuppositions and traditions, they can end up coming to some wrong conclusions. It's sad, and the havoc that has been caused in Christendom as a result of incorrect or false teachings is enormously regrettable.

However, I also think that there are those who want to see the church replace Israel simply because they are antisemites. Whether it's because of a bad upbringing, bad theology, bad history, bad character, or all of the above, they despise Jews and all things Jewish. When I write on social media about the antisemites of replacement theology or any other doctrinal positions not truly being Christians, these are the ones that I am talking about. How do I know an antisemite can't be a true believer? Because a true believer loves what God loves and hates what God hates. And, as we've already seen throughout this book, God's language toward Israel may be strong and He may bring tough discipline on the nation, but He has never and will never stop loving the Jewish people.

Without reading these verses through the lens of presupposition, there is no way to see them as Jesus making a blanket statement rejecting all Jews and assigning to them the appellation of "synagogue of Satan." It doesn't fit the immediate context, or the context of Revelation, and it certainly doesn't fit the overall context of Scripture.

God made a promise to Abraham. It was a promise without an exception or a caveat or an asterisk. "I will give you land. I will give you seed. I will make you a blessing." The only clarification the Lord made was to emphasize that the promise was not temporary, but would last forever (Genesis 13:14-15). By its eternal nature, we can be sure that the Lord's once-chosen people remain His chosen people.

Sadly, they remain in a state of rebellion, and that is not

something that God can abide, particularly if He wants to complete the pageant of His character. As a God of mercy, He needs the opportunity to show that mercy to Israel, bringing the people once and for all into His fold like chicks under His wings. How can He possibly pull that off? Don't worry, He has a plan, as we're about to see.

And for those of us in the church, how should we deal with Israel while the people are in this period of unbelief? The answer to that question is very simple, and it is found, not surprisingly, all the way back in the Israel Decree.

CHAPTER 5

TWO PEOPLE, TWO PLANS, ONE DESTINY

A great city stands before you. Its gates are opened wide, and through the gap, just a hint of the incredible architecture and lush greenery are visible. Laughter and singing reach your ears, bringing an irresistible smile to your face. Although you've never been here before, you know it's home. It just feels right. It is right.

But there is a problem. There's a wide trench between you and the city. It's difficult to see what exactly is down in the trench because the trees are tall and the ground is overgrown. You've heard about this trench and even read stories about it. It's dark and it can be arduous. However, you know that with hard work and a lot of effort you will assuredly reach the other side. Prepared to face the worst, you step toward the path that leads downward.

But before you take a second step, a hand grabs you. You turn and see a man standing behind you. There's a big smile on his face as he points to the right.

"Hey, friend, didn't you see that bridge over the trench? No need to go down there. We've got a smooth, wide path right over the top. God is good, isn't He?"

Gently, you remove the man's hand from your arm. Of course you had seen the bridge. Clean and covered with masses of people moving across it, you'd have to be blind to miss it. But those people were taking the easy way across. Access to the city was costing them nothing. In your mind, it was a blatant sign of disrespect to the mayor to simply stroll on in.

And that's what you told the man standing behind you.

You watched his brows furrow, knowing what was going to come next. You'd debated with people like him before, men and women who simply expected the rewards without all the work. Sure enough, he said, "But the mayor is the one who built the bridge. He did it so that we wouldn't have to go through the trench. Why wouldn't you take it?"

"You do it your way, and I'll do it mine, my friend. When we get inside, we'll see who gets the bigger house." As you turn and take the first steps down the rocky trail, you shake your head. *He'll learn*, you think. *Nothing good ever comes without a price.*

For those of you whose brains are working frantically right now trying to figure out why I just made a case for some people earning their salvation, you can relax. This is not a parable about working your way to heaven. It is, instead, a tale of modern-day Judaizing Christians who believe you have to become as Jewy of a Gentile believer as you possibly can. Because unless you follow the feasts and the kosher law, then God will never be quite as happy with you as He might have been if you had only put in a little more effort.

By the way, this also describes many of those who hold to the mid-tribulation and post-tribulation views of the rapture. If the Christians of ages past faced persecution, then why shouldn't we? If any period of the church needed a little smacking around to get it into shape, it's today's sad excuse for Christendom. But thankfully, our God is not an abuser, and He doesn't need His bride to have a black eye before she's ready for the marriage of the Lamb. Besides, there are plenty of parts of the world where the church is already experiencing terrible persecution. Even so, nowhere do the Scriptures state that the church needs a good bout of universal suffering before it will be ready to marry the Son. Instead of wishing pain upon ourselves, we should be praying that the Lord carries our struggling brothers and sisters through their difficulties. But all that is for another book.

Why do so many Christians want to be Jews? Why is there such an envy of this race of people who have suffered so many persecutions and pogroms and expulsions and holocausts? As a Jew, I can tell you that it isn't all duckies and bunnies. There is a price that comes with being one of God's chosen people. Besides, Gentiles wanting to be Jews is the exact opposite of what God intended. The Jews should not be provoking the Gentiles to jealousy, but the Gentiles should be provoking the Jews (Romans 11:11). Salvation came to the Jews first, but they rejected Him. Now, the gospel of salvation has come to the Gentile world. The time will come when it will once again return to the Jews, and that will be a wonderful day of revival.

AN IRREVOCABLE PROMISE

Still, I get it. There is something special about being of Israel. People know it. The world feels it. Why else has there never been a people more consistently dogpiled on throughout history? There is a uniqueness to Israel that the world can recognize. They just don't have the capability to ascertain its source. They may assign it to the sudden establishment of the State of Israel, and understandably so. Israel's creation stands out from that of other nations. God said,

> Who has heard such a thing?
>> Who has seen such things?
> Shall a land be born in one day?
>> Shall a nation be brought forth in one moment?
> For as soon as Zion was in labor
>> she brought forth her children (Isaiah 66:8 ESV).

God asked, "Can a nation be created in one day?" Then He answered yes by establishing Israel on May 14, 1948. An exclamation mark was added to the end of His affirmation when He miraculously routed all the nations that attempted to invade and destroy the country before it had a chance to take a breath.

Other people may believe the Jews' one-of-a-kind nature stems from Israel not always playing well with others. They seem to feel like they're special. Sort of like the seemingly unfounded arrogance of Nepal or Bhutan without all the monks or North Korea without the executions by piranha pool. It seems like Israel feels it's better than everyone else, a cut above.

But maybe the people of Israel actually are a cut above. I'm not talking in terms of quality or physicality or in any naturally quantifiable way. They are a cut above, or more accurately, a cut apart, because God chose them to be His "holy"—meaning "set apart"—nation (Exodus 19:6). They are special for the sole reason that God has declared them to be special. They are the physical fulfillment of the extraordinary promise He made thousands of years ago to an old man whose wife was well past childbearing age.

It is for this reason that Paul can be so emphatic in his words to the Romans. "I say then, has God cast away His people? Certainly not! For I also am an Israelite, of the seed of Abraham, of the tribe of Benjamin. God has not cast away His people whom He foreknew" (11:1-2). Not only *hasn't* God cast away His people, but He *can't* cast away His people. Because to do so would go against His character, against His longsuffering, merciful, *chesed* kind of love. And, as I said before, that truth is a huge affirmation for the church. We can know that as His spiritual children, He will never cast us away either. When God makes a promise, He keeps that promise forever and ever, amen!

Does that mean Israel has a special spiritual deal with God by which the people have received a unique path to salvation? Is justification by grace through faith only a new covenant deal or simply a plan for the Gentiles? Absolutely not. Again, back to Paul's words in Romans 11: "What then? Israel failed to obtain what it was seeking. The elect obtained it, but the rest were hardened" (verse 7 ESV). Israel, as a people, missed the close relationship they wanted with God by rejecting Yeshua when He was in their midst. Who received it instead? The elect, who, if you'll remember from a previous chapter, includes both Gentiles and Jews. Speaking as a Yeshua-following Jew, I'll raise my hand to testify to that.

Does this mean that all but a very small handful of believing Jews will face an eternity apart from God? Once again, Scripture demands that I answer in the negative. Paul wrote, "So I ask, did they stumble in order that they might fall? By no means! Rather, through their trespass salvation has come to the Gentiles, so as to make Israel jealous" (verse 11 ESV). Israel stumbled for a reason and only for a season. The people made their choice to reject Yeshua, so the Lord gave the salvific gospel to the Gentiles. But He did so with a purpose. Salvation came to the Gentiles in order to make Israel jealous. A reason like that comes with a built-in timeline because provoking to jealousy without an end game is worthless and cruel.

The hardening of Israel is not permanent and has not yet reached completion. A time is coming when the wall will break down and the Jewish people will finally be ready to receive Jesus as their Lord and Savior. "Lest you be wise in your own sight, I do not want you to be unaware of this mystery, brothers: a partial hardening has come upon Israel, until the fullness of the Gentiles has come in. And in this way all Israel will be saved" (verses 25-26 ESV). I know you have already read verse 26 numerous times in this book, but I can't help going back to it. This promise makes my heart soar! What an amazing testimony to our God and what an incredible commitment to His wayward children!

God has not replaced His children! As I wrote earlier, God cannot cast aside His chosen people so He can exchange them with another. That goes against who He is:

> As regards the gospel, they are enemies for your sake.
> But as regards election, they are beloved for the sake
> of their forefathers. For the gifts and the calling of

> God are irrevocable. For just as you were at one time
> disobedient to God but now have received mercy
> because of their disobedience, so they too have now
> been disobedient in order that by the mercy shown to
> you they also may now receive mercy (verses 28-31 ESV).

Read that passage again, then feel free to put the book down so you can jump up and dance or cheer or do a little jig. The gifts and calling of God are final, unchanging, immutable! We, Jews and Gentiles, were once lost in sin, but God took us into His family when we received Yeshua as our Lord and Savior. He called us to Him, He saved us, then He gave us spiritual gifts so we could serve Him. That will never change, and as a sign of our permanence in His family, He sealed us with His Holy Spirit.

> In Him you also trusted, after you heard the word
> of truth, the gospel of your salvation; in whom also,
> having believed, you were sealed with the Holy Spirit of
> promise, who is the guarantee of our inheritance until
> the redemption of the purchased possession, to the
> praise of His glory (Ephesians 1:13-14).

The Holy Spirit is our guarantee of salvation, an irrevocable promise that our eternity will be spent with the Lord. This pledge is available to all who receive Jesus as their Savior, both Jew and Gentile. For some reason, many people place Israel in a different salvation category than the rest of the world. But the Jewish people are in the same lost state everyone else once inhabited or still inhabits. But, praise the Lord, He has a plan to shake them out of their hedonism and spiritual lethargy. When He finally has their attention, they'll be ready to receive Him just as we did. They will experience the same mercy we experienced. They will be our brothers and sisters in Christ. What a day that will be!

HARD TIMES ARE COMING FOR ISRAEL

The path, however, to that glorious day of spiritual revival for Israel is going to be a bumpy one. At the end of the second-century Jewish revolt against Rome headed by Shimon Bar-Kokhba, Emperor Hadrian had had enough of the rebellious people of Jerusalem and of Israel as a whole. Jerusalem was destroyed and the land was plowed under. Jews were expelled from the city limits, and the area where the city formerly stood was renamed Aelia Capitolina. Because the persecution was so great, most Jews fled the land, with only a remnant staying behind. That's how the region stayed for centuries. At times the Jewish population grew, and at other times it waned. As the center of Judaism and the hub of Israel's people, Jerusalem ceased to have any pull.

But, as I mentioned earlier, God still had a plan for His holy nation and for His city. He began to prepare the land for the return of the people according to His promise. He said, "You, O mountains of Israel, shall shoot forth your branches and yield your fruit to my people Israel, for they will soon come home. For behold, I am for you, and I will turn to you, and you shall be tilled and sown. And I will multiply people on you, the whole house of Israel, all of it" (Ezekiel 36:8-10).

When the land was in a state of readiness for the hard work the returning exiles would bring, God began to call His people home. Once again, these were the same people of the physical line of Abraham, and their return was according to His promise:

> The nations will know that I am the LORD, declares the Lord GOD, when through you I vindicate my holiness before their eyes. I will take you from the nations and gather you from all the countries and bring you into your own land. I will sprinkle clean water on you, and you shall be clean from all your uncleannesses, and from all your idols I will cleanse you. And I will give you a new heart, and a new spirit I will put within you. And I will remove the heart of stone from your flesh and give you a heart of flesh. And I will put my Spirit within you, and cause you to walk in my statutes and be careful to obey my rules. You shall dwell in the land that I gave to your fathers, and you shall be my people, and I will be your God (verses 23-28 ESV).

Why does God do this? Is it because Israel is so wonderful? No, it's to vindicate His holiness. It's to demonstrate to the world who He is. And it's just as true today as it was when the people began to return in earnest at the beginning of the twentieth century. Modern Israel is continuing to carry out its part in the Lord's pageant of His character. How do I know that Ezekiel was talking about today and not when Israel returned from the exile? It's very simple. When has Israel ever had its heart of stone replaced with a heart of flesh? When has God's Spirit permeated its people? This didn't happen after the exile. And so far, it hasn't happened today. But the time is coming when we will see the hearts of Israel's people passionate for the true God.

If we continue to read Ezekiel, we see a promise that would have blown away the people of the prophet's day. When he saw the dry bones mentioned in chapter 37, Israel and Judah had been separated into two nations for hundreds of years. But God made a promise that when the dead bones had life breathed into them and the people came back and filled the land, they would do it as one nation, one Israel.

In 1949, Germany split and became two separate nations. Not only did a razor-wire border divide the two halves, but so did ideology. For decades, it was impossible to think of the two countries once again becoming one. But then on November 9, 1989, the Berlin Wall fell, and about a year later, on October 3, 1990, East Germany and West Germany united to become Germany. If you were alive at the time, I'm sure you can remember the wonder and amazement within Germany and around the world. How could two such disparate groups once again become one? In Ezekiel 37, that was exactly what God was promising to the two halves of His people who had been separated not for decades, but for centuries.

> The word of the LORD came to me: "Son of man, take a stick and write on it, 'For Judah, and the people of Israel associated with him'; then take another stick and write on it, 'For Joseph (the stick of Ephraim) and all the house of Israel associated with him.' And join them one to another into one stick, that they may become one in your hand...Thus says the Lord

GOD: Behold, I will take the people of Israel from the nations among which they have gone, and will gather them from all around, and bring them to their own land. And I will make them one nation in the land, on the mountains of Israel. And one king shall be king over them all, and they shall be no longer two nations, and no longer divided into two kingdoms" (verses 15-17, 21-22 ESV).

What a wonderful prophecy! What an amazing promise! When you look at the land of Israel today, you don't see tribal divisions. There is no longer a northern kingdom of Israel and a separate southern kingdom of Israel. We are reunited as Israelis, one united stick in the hand of the prophet. It's incredible what God can do!

If only the story had ended there. But it couldn't. God had promised new hearts for the people of Israel. But He doesn't force righteousness onto any person. When the Jews came back to Israel, they did so physically, but spiritually, they were still a long way off. The Holy Spirit could tickle that trigger in the Jewish mind so that their bodies started moving home. It was up to the people to offer up their hearts.

Thus, we come to Ezekiel 38. Israel is finally at peace. The October 7 War is over. People can go outside without having to watch out for exploding drones or falling pieces of missiles. The population of the State of Israel is finally in a place of contentment and prosperity that they have desired ever since they declared independence in 1948. Unfortunately, like all good things in this natural world, this will not last.

Way up in the far north, Russia will be looking down on Israel with ruble signs in their eyes. It could be the Jewish state's incredible technology that draws Moscow's attention. Or maybe the near-miraculous agricultural inventions Israel has come up with. But because Russia is an energy economy, the pull will most likely come from the vast natural gas fields that Israel owns just off the Mediterranean coast. Red Square will call up the presidential palace in Ankara, Turkey, and the Supreme Leader's residence in Tehran, Iran, and ask, "Hey, you guys up for a rumble in Israel?"

This is what we find in Ezekiel 38:

> Thus says the Lord God: "Behold, I am against you, O Gog, the prince of Rosh, Meshech, and Tubal. I will turn you around, put hooks into your jaws, and lead you out, with all your army, horses, and horsemen, all splendidly clothed, a great company with bucklers and shields, all of them handling swords. Persia, Ethiopia, and Libya are with them, all of them with shield and helmet; Gomer and all its troops; the house of Togarmah from the far north and all its troops—many people are with you…On that day when My people Israel dwell safely, will you not know it? Then you will come from your place out of the far north, you and many peoples with you, all of them riding on horses, a great company and a mighty army. You will come up against My people Israel like a cloud, to cover the land. It will be in the latter days that I will bring you against My land, so that the nations

may know Me, when I am hallowed in you, O Gog, before their eyes" (verses 3-6, 14-16).

Through the avarice that is already in the hearts of Russia's leaders, God will allow the Russian army to unite with Persia (Iran), Ethiopia (Sudan), Libya, and Gomer and Togarmah (Turkey) against Israel. This will be a vast, powerful army that will be impossible to stop, no matter how well stocked the defenses of the Iron Dome, David's Sling, and Arrow might be. On paper, Israel is destined to be routed. But, as they say in American football, that's why you play the game.

> "I will call for a sword against Gog throughout all My mountains," says the Lord GOD. "Every man's sword will be against his brother. And I will bring him to judgment with pestilence and bloodshed; I will rain down on him, on his troops, and on the many peoples who are with him, flooding rain, great hailstones, fire, and brimstone. Thus I will magnify Myself and sanctify Myself, and I will be known in the eyes of many nations. Then they shall know that I am the LORD" (verses 21-23).

Mann tracht, un Gott lacht is an old Yiddish proverb that means "Man plans, and God laughs." The unstoppable army will be stopped cold. But it won't be by jets or bombs or ground forces. God will make it very clear that this battle is His, and the victory will come from His hands. You don't have to do a deep theological dive to discover His reason for letting Russia and friends attack so that they can be subsequently decimated. God tells us in a phrase that is found throughout the book of Ezekiel: "Then they shall know that I am the LORD."

Remember the whole reason for creation. God is showing who He is, and part of showing *who* He is includes demonstrating *that* He is. To riff off of Psalm 20:7, Russia and company will trust in chariots and horses, but the Lord will show that it is in His name that all should trust.

There are those who believe that the war Ezekiel spoke of already took place when God brought the well-deserved judgment upon Babylon. "There's no need for some future war that leads to a seven-year tribulation." But the Lord Himself negated that possibility when He said to Gog, "Are you he of whom I have spoken in former days by My servants the prophets of Israel, who prophesied for years in those days that I would bring you against them?" (Ezekiel 38:17). First, Ezekiel was a prophet during the Babylonian exile, and the others who prophesied regarding Babylon's destruction were not so far back that they would be considered of "former days." Second, in the context of Ezekiel 38, there is no destruction of Israel followed decades later by a retaliatory destruction against the attackers as we see in the case of Babylon. Instead, there is an invasion that is thwarted. The only ways for such vast armies to be repulsed so quickly and completely is to either allegorize the whole incident or to look for a future fulfillment.

The only time to interpret a passage allegorically is when Scripture makes it clear that it is an allegory. This is not that kind of passage. In fact, it's exactly the opposite. Does the world need a clearer example of God's existence than Him supernaturally decimating an army that is invading His land? Could the people of

Israel possibly require additional demonstrations that God is real and wants a relationship with them?

Sadly, the answer for both the world and for Israel is yes. Because the Ezekiel War takes place at the launch of the tribulation, there will still be seven years to go before "all Israel will be saved" (Romans 11:26). In the aftermath of the onslaught and defeat of the mighty army of the north and east and south, a man will arise promising peace. Many will be skeptical at first, particularly those in Israel. God had just done the impossible; who needs some upstart European guy to suddenly start telling everyone what they need to do? But then this political leader will match God by carrying out an impossible work of his own. He will negotiate a deal that will allow the Jews to rebuild the temple. Who could possibly accomplish a feat of that political, social, and religious magnitude if the Lord were not on his side? The Jews, as well as millions of others around the globe, will attach themselves to this social genius like lint to Velcro.

It will be hard to blame the population for their adoration. Anyone who can bring stability during such a time would be lauded as a hero. What people won't realize is that this man, the Antichrist, won't come alone. When his time begins, so will the tribulation period. For seven years, the world will shake like it's never been shaken before.

When the tribulation starts, the globe will quickly become a very different place than it is now. The defeat of the Russian axis will be the first supernatural event of many more to come. The seal judgments found in Revelation 6 will shake up the world, and there will be widespread wars, violence, food shortages, plagues, and meteors causing massive numbers of deaths. Through it all, the Antichrist will stand tall and give hope to the masses. No wonder all eyes will turn to him. But this great hero who seems to the world to be a latter-day savior will actually be demonic. He will bide his time at first, then will show his true colors.

In the middle of the seven years of the tribulation, the peace-loving mask of the Antichrist will come off:

> He shall confirm a covenant with many for
>   one week;
> but in the middle of the week
> he shall bring an end to sacrifice and offering.
> And on the wing of abominations shall be one
>   who makes desolate,
> even until the consummation, which is determined,
> is poured out on the desolate (Daniel 9:27).

The Antichrist will put an end to Jewish sacrifice in the rebuilt temple and instead demand worship of himself, setting up an "abomination of desolation" (12:11) in the holy structure. Jesus spoke to His disciples of this time as they sat on the Mount of Olives. He said,

> "When you see the 'abomination of desolation,' spoken
> of by Daniel the prophet, standing in the holy place"
> (whoever reads, let him understand), "then let those
> who are in Judea flee to the mountains...For then
> there will be great tribulation, such as has not been
> since the beginning of the world until this time, no,
> nor ever shall be. And unless those days were shortened,

no flesh would be saved; but for the elect's sake those
days will be shortened" (Matthew 24:15-16, 21-22).

Those in Israel who are wise will heed those words given 2,000
years ago. Those who don't? Zechariah wrote of them:

"It shall come to pass in all the land,"
  says the LORD,
"That two-thirds in it shall be cut off and die,
  but one-third shall be left in it:
  I will bring the one-third through the fire,
  will refine them as silver is refined,
  and test them as gold is tested.
  They will call on My name,
  and I will answer them.
  I will say, 'This is My people';
  and each one will say, 'The LORD is my God'"
  (13:8-9).

It is heart-wrenching to know that two out of every three
people that I see around me as I go about my daily life in Israel
will not survive the tribulation. There will be a horrific slaughter
like we've never seen, even during the Holocaust and on October 7. That is why, for my own sanity, I need to focus on the second half of that promise. One-third of my people will survive
the seven years of Jacob's trouble. They will be beaten and battered, refined and tested as if they were precious metals. These
are the ones who will see Yeshua when He returns. These are the
penitents whom the Lord spoke of through Zechariah just one

chapter earlier, saying, "They will look on Me whom they pierced. Yes, they will mourn for Him as one mourns for his only son, and grieve for Him as one grieves for a firstborn" (12:10). This is that wonderful group of Jewish revivalists of whom Paul was speaking when he wrote—and I bet you can say it with me by now—"and so all Israel will be saved" (Romans 11:26).

"But, Amir, now you're saying that people should be beaten and battered before they are united with the Lord. Why isn't that true of the church?" Yes, that is what I'm saying, but there is a difference between Israel and the church. Israel is in rebellion, and the tribulation is God's period of tough love to bring the people to repentance. It is what is needed to soften their hearts so that they are ready to receive Yeshua as their Messiah. Salvation, however, has already come to the church. We have repented and are now right with God. What purpose would the church suffering through the tribulation accomplish other than forcing believers to go through a real-world purgatory to help pay for sins that Jesus already died for?

There are difficult days ahead for the people of Israel. But we Jews can take solace in knowing that thousands of years ago, God made a promise to us. He gave us land, He gave us a heritage, and He gave us a blessing. The Lord is faithful. He will deliver on that decree. My prayer is that many of my fellow Israelis will come to faith now while there is time before they have to experience God's convincing.

A TO-DO LIST FOR THE CHURCH

As much as I wish that there would be thousands, or even hundreds, in Israel who will read this book, I think that is highly unlikely. The readership for what I have written will primarily be among those in the church. So I don't want to leave the church without a plan of action. Like Paul, I've finished giving you all the *what*; now it's time for the *so what?* There are three key items on the church's to-do list when it comes to the Jews.

The church must celebrate Israel. That miraculous, born-in-a-day state is a living testimony of the surety of God's promises and the longsuffering nature of His *chesed* love. These people were chosen and miraculously birthed by God. There were great periods over the years during which the people loved their Father and served Him with all their hearts. There were many more times when they didn't, including, for the most part, today.

But whether in good times or in bad, God's love never wavered. During the times of blessings for their faithfulness or curses for their rebellion, He never changed. Once again, the love of God for Israel is proof positive of the comprehensive and unwavering hope that we in the church can put in our salvation through the Messiah. If God had let Israel go, we'd have to wonder where the line was between our continued salvation and being jettisoned from the family. But because He held onto them as His people despite all their sin, we can be assured that He will always hold onto us as His children.

So rejoice in Israel. Bring out your Israeli flags. Circle up with the Bible study group that meets in your home to dance and sing "Hava Nagila." Bring a couple dozen chocolate rugelach and some halva to your church potluck. God's love never fails, and His promises are irrevocable.

Another item for the church's to-do list is to give financially to Israel. When Paul was beginning his sign-off to the Romans, he commended the primarily Gentile churches of Macedonia and Achaia for collecting a gift for the poor Jewish believers in Jerusalem. He claimed this to be only right, "for if the Gentiles have been partakers of [the Jews'] spiritual things, their duty is also to minister to them in material things" (Romans 15:27). As benefactors of the spiritual blessings of the Israel Decree, the church has a responsibility to minister to the physical needs of those who are hurting in Israel itself.

As of the time I'm writing this, there are still tens of thousands of Israelis who are out of their homes due to the war. This is in both the south near Gaza and in the north by Lebanon and Syria. The government is taking care of them the best it can, but many still need help with basic needs.

Since October 7, 2023, the tourist industry in Israel has also taken a devastating hit. Not too many foreigners are excited about sightseeing around a war zone. Tour companies, hotels, gift shops, restaurants, bus companies—all are experiencing severe trials, and many have had to shut down. Even a small economic infusion would be enough to keep some afloat.

This is also true of Israel's internal charities. Many Israelis are struggling just to get by. As a result, their charitable giving has waned. This has led to hard times for organizations that reach out to orphans, various types of victims, and the homeless. The ravages of war are not only on the front lines. They permeate throughout society.

The Israel Decree given to Abraham said that God would bless those who bless him and his descendants. This shows His love for Abraham's progeny and His dependence upon others to come alongside His people when help is needed. This was true in the past, it is true now, and it will continue to be true in the times to come. The prophet Joel wrote of a judgment when the Gentiles who survive the tribulation will be gathered together for adjudication based on how they treated Israel. Through the prophet, God said, "Behold, in those days and at that time, when I bring back the captives of Judah and Jerusalem, I will also gather all nations, and bring them down to the Valley of Jehoshaphat; and I will enter into judgment with them there on account of My people, My heritage Israel" (Joel 3:1-2). Jesus spoke of this same judgment, setting it into a future context, when He taught about the separation of the sheep from the goats.

> When the Son of Man comes in His glory, and all the holy angels with Him, then He will sit on the throne of His glory. All the nations will be gathered before Him, and He will separate them one from another, as a shepherd divides his sheep from the goats (Matthew 25:31-32).

What will the criteria look like for making it into the cherished sheep side? It won't be complicated. That flock will be reserved for those who sacrificially gave what they could to the needy. And who were these needy? Jesus said, "Assuredly, I say to you, inasmuch as you did it to one of the least of these My brethren, you did it to Me" (verse 40). Jesus' brethren, otherwise known as the Jews.

Finally, and most importantly, please pray for Israel. If the war is still going on when you read this, pray for a soon peace that ensures the safety of the Israeli people. Pray for wisdom for our leaders and protection from outside forces. Pray for unity among the people as certain segments within the government and the media seem to be doing their best to fracture our nation. Pray for the peace of Jerusalem.

Most of all, though, pray for the salvation of the people of Israel. As I mentioned earlier in this chapter, two out of every three people whom I pass on the road from Behold Israel's CONNECT office to my home will not survive the tribulation. They need the Messiah now! Please pray for a revival within my country, a movement of the Holy Spirit before the church is raptured away from this earth. I know that the veil still rests on most hearts, but I am evidence that the Holy Spirit can lift that veil off any heart and draw that person to Himself.

So pray, my brothers and sisters. Know that as you are pouring out your prayers of blessing upon the people of God, He is taking notice. Thus, you can be assured that as a father smiles with contentment when he sees his children loving each other, the Lord is watching you with great joy.

The Israel of today is no different than the Israel of the Bible. It is the same land filled with the same people who have been given the same blessings. But the same enemy who has always been there continues to lurk, trying to convince you otherwise. Instead of falling into his trap of doubt and uncertainty, celebrate the faithful God whose promises never change.

NOTES

1. Justin Martyr, "Saint Justin Martyr (110-165): Dialogue with Trypho," *Logos Library*, https://www.logoslibrary.org/justin/trypho/011.html.

2. Justin Martyr, "Dialogue with Trypho (chapters 125–142)," *New Advent*, https://www.newadvent.org/fathers/01289.htm.

3. Irenaeus, "Against Heresies (Book III, Chapter 21)," *New Advent*, https://www.newadvent.org/fathers/0103321.htm.

4. Origen, "Contra Celsum, Book IV," *New Advent*, https://www.newadvent.org/fathers/04164.htm.

5. John Chrysostom, "John Chrysostom (c. 347–407): Eight Homilies Against the Jews, Homily 1," https://www.laits.utexas.edu/bodian/la-johnChrysostom.html.

6. Fr. Vasile Mihoc, "St Paul and the Jews According to St John Chrysostom's Commentary on Romans 9-11," PDF download, https://www.vanderbilt.edu/AnS/religious_studies/SBL2007/Mihoc.pdf.

7. "Anti-Semitism: Martin Luther—'The Jews & Their Lies,'" *Jewish Virtual Library*, https://www.jewishvirtuallibrary.org/martin-luther-quot-the-jews-and-their-lies-quot.

8. "Is There Unknown Antisemitism in Your Theology?," *Gateway Center for Israel*, https://centerforisrael.com/article/is-there-unknown-anti-semitism-in-your-theology/.

9. John Piper, "Israel, Palestine, and the Middle East," *desiringGod*, March 7, 2004, https://www.desiringgod.org/messages/israel-palestine-and-the-middle-east.

10. Mark Twain, *The Innocents Abroad* (Waxkeep Publishing, 2013), 212, Kindle edition.

11. See https://www.jewishvirtuallibrary.org/the-first-aliyah-1882-1903.

12. See https://www.history.com/this-day-in-history/britain-and-france-conclude-sykes-picot-agreement.

13. "Balfour Declaration," *The Avalon Project, Yale Law School*, https://avalon.law.yale.edu/20th_century/balfour.asp.

14. "San Remo Resolution-Palestine Mandate 1920," *MidEastWeb*, http://mideastweb.org/san_remo_palestine_1920.htm.

15. "The Hamas Covenant," *Israel*, https://embassies.gov.il/holysee/AboutIsrael/the-middle-east/Pages/The%20Hamas-Covenant.aspx.

16. "The Palestine Mandate," *The Avalon Project, Yale Law School*, https://avalon.law.yale.edu/20th_century/palmanda.asp.

17. "Charter of the United Nations," Chapter XII, Article 80, *Repertory of Practice of United Nations Organs*, https://legal.un.org/repertory/art80.shtml.

18. "WAFA: 'Number of Palestinians worldwide doubled 10 times since Nakba, official figures show,'" *IMEMC News*, May 15, 2022, https://imemc.org/article/wafa-number-of-palestinians-worldwide-doubled-10-times-since-nakba-official-figures-show/.

OTHER GREAT HARVEST HOUSE
BOOKS BY AMIR TSARFATI

In *Israel and the Church*, bestselling author and native Israeli Amir Tsarfati helps readers recognize the distinct contemporary and future roles of both the Jewish people and the church, and how together they reveal the character of God and His perfect plan of salvation.

To fully grasp what God has in store for the future, it's vital to understand His promises to Israel. The *Israel and the Church Study Guide* will help you do exactly that, equipping you to explore the Bible's many revelations about what is yet to come.

Amir Tsarfati, with Dr. Rick Yohn, examines what Revelation makes known about the end times and beyond. Guided by accessible teaching that lets Scripture speak for itself, you'll see what lies ahead for every person in the end times—either in heaven or on earth. Are *you* ready?

This companion workbook to *Revealing Revelation*—the product of many years of careful research—offers you a clear and exciting overview of God's perfect plan for the future. Inside you'll find principles from the Bible that equip you to better interpret the end-times signs, as well as insights about how Bible prophecy is relevant to your life today.

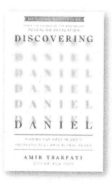

Discovering Daniel reveals how the words, actions, and visions of the prophet Daniel can provide you with purpose and hope in today's chaotic world, encouraging you to live with confidence in God's supreme sovereignty and love in the time we have left on this earth. In this book, you'll also explore the deep connection between Daniel and Revelation.

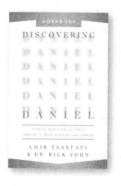

In a culture fraught with fear and discord, Bible prophecy helps soothe our anxious hearts while deepening our trust in God's providence and care. The *Discovering Daniel Workbook* will help you apply the remarkable insights of Daniel to your daily life, emboldening you to live with hope and confidence.

As a native Israeli of Jewish roots, Amir Tsarfati provides a distinct perspective that weaves biblical history, current events, and Bible prophecy together to shine light on the mysteries about the end times. In *The Day Approaching*, he points to the scriptural evidence that the return of the Lord is imminent.

Jesus Himself revealed the signs that will alert us to the nearness of His return. In *The Day Approaching Study Guide*, you'll have the opportunity to take an up-close look at what those signs are, as well as God's overarching plans for the future, and how those plans affect you today.

Bestselling author and native Israeli Amir Tsarfati provides clarity on what will happen during the tribulation and explains its place in God's timeline.

With this study guide companion to *Has the Tribulation Begun?*, bestselling author and prophecy expert Amir Tsarfati guides you through a biblical overview of the last days, with thought-provoking study and application questions.

AMIR TSARFATI
WITH BARRY STAGNER

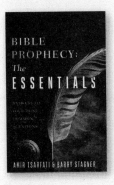

In *Bible Prophecy: The Essentials*, Amir and Barry team up to answer 70 of their most commonly asked questions, which focus on seven foundational themes of Bible prophecy: Israel, the church, the rapture, the tribulation, the millennium, the Great White Throne judgment, and heaven.

AMIR TSARFATI
WITH STEVE YOHN

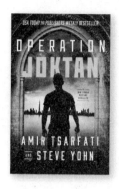

BOOK 1

A terrorist attack brings Nir and Nicole together, and then work forces them apart—until they're unexpectedly called back into each other's lives. But there's no time for romance. As violent radicals threaten chaos across the Middle East, the two must work to stop these extremists, pooling Nicole's knack for technology and Nir's adeptness with on-the-ground missions. Each heart-racing step of their operation gets them closer to the truth—and closer to danger.

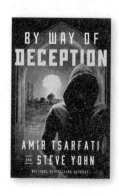

BOOK 2

Nir and Nicole find themselves caught in a whirlwind plot of assassinations, espionage, and undercover recon, fighting against the clock to stop this threat against the Middle East. As they draw closer to danger—and closer to each other—they find themselves ensnared in a lethal web of secrets. Will they have to sacrifice their own lives to protect the lives of millions?

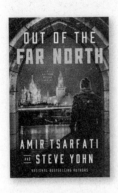

BOOK 3

Israel discovers that Russia is secretly planning an attack against it—but has no idea when and how. In the race to prevent a devastating conflict, will Mossad agents Nir Tavor and Nicole le Roux be able to outwit their enemies—or will their actions have catastrophic consequences?

BOOK 4

With Israel's energy future at stake and deadly adversaries uniting against the country, Nir and his team face their most dangerous battle for survival against forces determined to see the Jewish nation fall.